LONDON TALES

For Betty

best wishes,

Terry

ALSO BY TERENCE JENKINS:

Another Man's London

London Lives

'Return': A Collection of Short Stories

Co-Author of 'The Book of Penge, Anerley & Crystal Palace"

LONDON TALES

TERENCE JENKINS

Copyright © 2012 Terence Jenkins

The right of Terence Jenkins to be identified as the Author of the Work has been asserted by him in accordance with the Copyright, Designs and Patents Act 1998

This book is sold subject to the condition it shall not, by way of trade or otherwise, be lent, resold, hired out, or otherwise circulated in any form or by any means, electronic or otherwise without the publisher's prior consent.

A catalogue record for this book is available from the British Library

ISBN 978-1-909121-03-4

Published by
Acorn Independent Press
www.acornselfpublishing.com

To those who take the road less travelled

CONTENTS

Scandal in Strand	1
Dug Up Twice	7
Angels and Romans on the Rye	13
Palimpsest	19
Carry On, Whitehall	23
Absolutely Fabulous in Cheam	31
The Harvest of the Sea	35
The One-Way Ticket Railway	41
From Bootleg Bibles to Bedpans	45
Heads and Tales	51
Cheaper by the Cartload	57
In a Monastery Garden	63
The African Roscius	69
Coade	73
A Chaotic Quarter of Ruffianism	79
Dickens and the Borough	87
England's Michelanglo and the Unsung Heroes	93
The Lord Mayor's Daughter and the Crossing Sweeper	97
Somewhat of a Cockney	101
One Street	107
Keeping Faith	113
Where Wolves Preyed on the Thames Bank	119
London's Lobby	123
Fulham Palace and its Gardens	131
From Shimla to the South Circular	137
Homes R Us	141
Snail Mail and Rowland Hill	147
Crocodiles, Pelicans and a Boozy Elephant	151
A Passion for Collecting	157
Drunk for a Penny, Dead Drunk for Two Pence	161

Scandal in Strand

My paternal grandmother, Alice, a widow, and her sister, Gertie, married to Uncle Alf, used to have a routine which kept us kids entertained at Christmas time when the whole family descended on one or the other. After the festive lunch had been eaten and everything cleared away, we would go into the front-room and Uncle Alf would open up the piano lid and a good old sing-song would begin. As well as Christmas carols there would be some music-hall songs popular with the industrial working class. We would belt out *My Old Man Said Follow the Van*, *Hello! Hello! Who's your Lady Friend?*, *My Old Dutch* and others but our favourite was *Let's All Go Down the Strand* which was sung as a duet by the two matriarchs and the rest of us would join in the chorus of "Have a banana" with gusto. Once, I asked, "What's the Strand?" to be told, "It's a posh street in London." Its "poshness" was further established by another song we sang, *Burlington Bertie*, the Toff who would "walk down the Strand with his gloves on his hand/and walk back again with them off." The street gained almost mythic status in my young mind.

Strand, (for that is its name, there is no definite article), stretches for three-quarters of a mile from Charing Cross to the Law Courts, right up to where the City of London begins, which was once marked by Temple Bar on which criminals heads were exhibited stuck on poles after they'd been dipped in pitch to make their exhibition last longer and to prevent the crows from devouring them too quickly. The street in WC2 joins the political centre of power to the financial. It once ran along the edge of the Thames and was called the Strandway in the eleventh century when it was originally a bridle path much closer to the river, centuries before Bazalgette built the Victoria Embankment.

At the height of its "poshness", along its length could be found the great mansions and palaces of rich and powerful nobles such as Essex House, Somerset House and, grandest of all, the Palace of the Savoy where John of Gaunt kept court. When the Royal Court was in the east of town, the nobles wanted to be near the seat of power, but when it moved west so did they and thus began the change to the area. At one stage it fell so far from fashion that it was known for being full of "coffee houses, low taverns and cheap women". The Dog and Duck was a tavern where the Gunpowder conspirators met and at The Coal Hole there were evenings of notorious ribaldry.

Once a residential street, it was home to many famous folk: Sarah Siddons, the actress lived at No. 149; George Eliot, the novelist at 142; Samuel Taylor Coleridge, the poet at 348; and R. L. Stevenson's Dr. Jekyll banked at Coutts, 440 Strand.

At one time there were more theatres in its length than on any other street in London but now only the Adelphi, the Savoy and the Vaudeville remain among the shops, restaurants and hotels. There are two beautiful churches towards its eastern end, St. Mary-le-Strand and St. Clement Danes and a few statues, including Dr. Johnson and "Bomber" Harris, the controversial RAF commander, but perhaps the most interesting building is Zimbabwe House, the embassy of that African nation at 429 Strand.

Originally, this building on the corner with Agar Street was the headquarters of the British Medical Association which, in 1905, commissioned the young sculptor, Jacob Epstein (1880-1959) to carve 18 figures, eight feet high, to adorn its façade. What they had in mind was a row of figures of famous medical men. However, what they got, after Epstein voiced his disagreement with them, was something totally different. The 27 year-old sculptor's choice was to cause some scandal in Strand and nationally.

Epstein said that he would carve "noble and heroic forms to express in sculpture the great primal acts of man and woman". It follows that these acts, if they were to have any authenticity, should be, mainly, naked bodies for he believed that "we are too ashamed of our nakedness". There then, eventually, appeared a sequence of nude men and women symbolising the ages of Man. There was much controversy among the Edwardian public who were offended not simply by the nakedness of the figures but also by certain features: an old woman cradling a baby was shown with withered breasts; the figure of Maternity was a young woman whose nakedness was too obvious for the times; and to cap it all, a young man whose virility left little to the imagination as he stood full-frontal to the street. Uproar all round from the scandalised self-righteous. One newspaper said that they were "statuary no father would wish his daughter or no young man, his fiancée to see."

"Day" by Jacob Epstein – above St. James' Park Underground Station. Both the statues which were carved in situ caused controversy and claims of pagan obscenity and paedophilia. At the time, protestors tarred and feathered them. Epstein was forced to truncate the child's penis.

Across the street was the National Vigilance Society, which, apocryphal tales tell, had to cover its windows so that the employees would not be so shocked that they couldn't get on with their work guarding the nation's morals. One member, Father Bernard Vaughan, claimed the right not to have such anatomical correctness "thrust" at him or the "sacred subject of maternity" traduced by such "brutal commonplace" representations of the human form. Needless to say, people, mainly young girls and young men, gathered in their hundreds to see what was causing all the fuss. Heigh-ho, 'twas ever thus. Even the police were called to the scene.

The British Medical Association had second thoughts but Epstein was allowed to continue with his work when he gained the support of art critics, museum directors, and fellow sculptors. The finished statues were allowed to remain. But not for long, as the controversy broke out again. In 1935 the BMA left the building and the Government of Southern Rhodesia moved in. They claimed that the figures were decaying and needed replacing. Once again the philistines were joined in battle with supporters of Epstein's work who won the day. The statues remained in place.

However, as though Fate were conspiring against them, they were covered up for the Coronation Procession of King George VI in 1937 and, after the celebrations were over, as the bunting, flags etc. were being taken down, a piece of one of the statues broke off and fell to the ground, narrowly missing a passer-by. Of course, wags claimed it was a falling penis, which gave rise to much ribaldry. One joker, it is said, put up a notice saying, "Beware Falling Phalluses" and another said that the building "Gave him the willies". The London County Council issued a safety order to make the statues safe. Epstein, himself, offered to do the work but this was turned down. The President of the Royal Academy, among others, inspected them and the conclusion was reached that all bits – limbs, heads and genitalia – that might fall down in future were to be chiselled away. This sanctioned vandalism so appalled Henry Moore that he vowed never to exhibit at the Academy.

The statues were duly "rectified" and there they remain to this day, savaged by hypocrisy, mere shells of their former selves, unnoticed by today's passers-by who are unaware of the subject of such cultural controversy above their heads. If you want to see other examples of Epstein's work that caused problems look at the figures of Night and Day over the entrances to St. James' Park tube station. These, too, caused uproar. Some claimed they were un-Christian and glorified pagan deities. Others said they had undertones of paedophilia. At one stage, outraged students tarred and feathered them. In an effort to pacify the easily outraged, Epstein cut a few inches off the boy's penis on Day. Honour was satisfied and there they remain.

In Hyde Park, north of the Serpentine, is Epstein's memorial to the naturalist W. H. Hudson, the stone relief of Rima, the heroine of the book, *Green Mansions*. When poor old Stanley Baldwin, the Prime Minister, unveiled this amply bare-breasted woman, he was so embarrassed, that he fled the scene. There are other, less controversial examples of Epstein's work in London: the figure of Field Marshall Smuts in Parliament Square who appears to be skating; the Madonna and Child in Cavendish Square; and the Pieta in Congress House, Bloomsbury. They are all worth seeing for it would be a shame if this influential figure in modern sculpture were to be remembered only for the mutilated figures and falling phallus in Strand.

Dug Up Twice

The Bayswater Road, London postal district W2, is one of the more pleasant main roads in London. Once a turnpike road and still tree-lined, it runs north of Hyde Park along the route of what was once the Roman Via Tribantia. To the east, after Marble Arch (which once stood in front of Buckingham Palace and through which only senior members of the Royal Family and the Queen's Troop Royal Horse Artillery may pass) it becomes the consumers' paradise of Oxford Street and to the west it leads to fashionable Notting Hill. Sir James Barrie lived at No. 100, where he wrote *Peter Pan*, and somewhere along its length lived Galsworthy's fictional Forsyte family of the eponymous saga and hugely popular TV show. On the opposite side of the road, hanging from the railings of Hyde Park can be seen on Sundays between 10 a. m. – 6 p. m. what has been called the longest open-air art show in Europe.

Not far west of the Bayswater Road's junction with the Edgware Road is St. George's Fields, a 1970's housing development of 300 desirable apartments in a most attractive garden square (sometimes open on Open Squares Day in June) which can only be glimpsed from the main road but which has a minor but strange, tangential role in English literary history.

Shady Hall, Coxwold, where Laurence Sterne lived

As you might surmise, St. George's Fields derives its name from a church, but where is it? St. George, Hanover Square, one of the 50 new churches proposed by the Act of 1711, is about half a mile away at the Bond Street end of Mayfair. It is posh and its opulent interior is a popular venue for society weddings. At one time it was so crowded with aristocracy that James Boswell had to leave because his "eyes were too much attracted to the Duchess of Grafton". Disraeli was married there, as were George Eliot, Marconi and Theodore Roosevelt. The large classical portico (the first of its kind in London) dominates the street but there is very little outside space attached to the church. Where did they bury their dead?

The first burial ground is a little way apart in Mount Street where the one and a half acre site soon filled up and is now an enclosed park laid out as a public garden, maintained by the vestry. The tombstones have been used to retain the flanking slopes and, in Summer, the tall plane trees make it a welcome haven from the heat in summer.

However, this filled up quickly and in 1736 a five acre site was bought on the Bayswater Road, opposite what was then the open countryside that became Hyde Park. By 1854 this too had become full and the Board of Health recommended it be closed because, it claimed, there were body parts hanging in the trees and barrow loads of decomposing bodies were being tipped into a pit. Despite this, the incumbent claimed there was room for more: no doubt he was mindful of the revenues brought in by burials. And it is in such conditions that we begin to find the literary link.

Laurence Sterne (1713-68), called "the father of the English novel", although born in Ireland, was brought up and educated in England where he attended Halifax Grammar School and Jesus College, Oxford. He became a country parson in Sutton-on-Forest in Yorkshire from where he produced, in 1759, the first two volumes of *The Life and Times of Tristram Shandy, Gentleman* which was such a success, that he was offered the living of Coxwold, a very attractive village in the beautiful area of the Hambleton and Howardian Hills. He wrote seven more volumes of Shandy's adventures, which added to his fame.

His work was not the kind of thing expected of a clergyman, being bawdy, humorous and meandering but it caught the public imagination, especially among the educated and society classes in the capital and he visited London a number of times, where he was fêted.

Sterne had never had a strong constitution and suffered from consumption (tuberculosis) most of his life, but he was of an optimistic and cheerful disposition, believing, "every

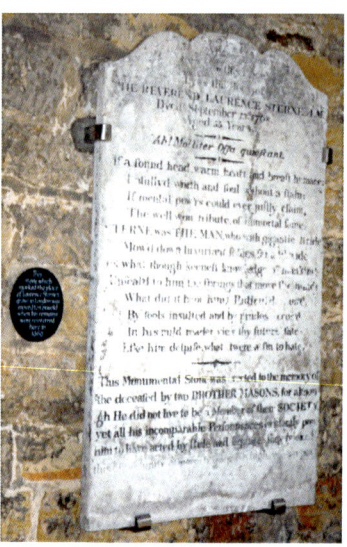

Laurence Sterne's gravestone which was moved from London to Coxwold in 1969 when his remains were reinterred

time a man smiles – but much more so when he laughs, it adds something to this Fragment of Life." What a splendid philosophy to live by.

In 1768, on a visit to London, he contracted pleurisy and died in seedy lodgings in Bond Street and a sad story is told that while he lay dying, his covetous landlady cut off his gold sleeve buttons. But even worse was to befall him.

This was the high period of bodysnatching, when corpses, preferably fresh ones, were dug up, dismembered and sold to students at medical schools for a profit – some were used in anatomy lectures. The school at Cambridge was a regular customer, for such cadavers and paid more for those dug up in winter because the cold weather preserved corpses for longer. Many measures were taken to deter the Resurrection

Men (sounds like a pop-group, doesn't it?), but nothing seemed to work, not the watchmen with dogs who patrolled the graveyards (at one such burial place even the dog was stolen), nor high walls or man-traps, and poor old Sterne, within days of his funeral, was dug up and transported by nefarious means to Cambridge where he ended up on a slab. It is claimed that when the body was unveiled ready for dissection someone there recognised him. Some say it was the Professor of Anatomy himself who had met Sterne at a social function in London and recognised the distinguished cadaver. Whoever it was, the body was quickly covered up and secretly returned to St. George's burial ground in the Bayswater Road where a headstone and footstone were later erected.

Over the next century, the cemetery became full and fell into disuse. At one stage during the First World War it became allotments. With the growing need for housing in London, it was cleared in 1969 in order that flats might be built, but not before the Laurence Sterne Trust had searched for Sterne's body.

There were complications for five skulls were found in the grave. Which was Sterne's? Joseph Nollekens, the famous sculptor, was able to provide the answer. A contemporary of the author, he had taken meticulous measurements for a bust of Sterne. When these were compared with the skulls, the correct one was found, reunited with the remains, and transferred to Coxwold where the author was reburied in the graveyard of his own church. A strange but satisfactory ending and one that Sterne, dug up twice, would have found amusing, I'm sure.

Angels and Romans on the Rye

Before the Normans arrived in 1066, the south-east corner of what is now the London Borough of Southwark, the second oldest London borough after the City, with an area of 2,888 hectares and a population of 230,000 was known to its inhabitants as Pecheha and as such is mentioned in the Doomsday Book, one of the foundations of the feudal system with its inventory of who owned what. The name is derived from the Anglo-Saxon for "hill". Therefore Peckham means "the village among the hills" and when you see Honour Oak Hill, Sydenham Hill and Nunhead nearby, it is easy to see why. A stream known locally as the Peck once flowed across Peckham Rye but it is now culverted and all that can be seen is its bed in the Park.

It was a small village in a rural area surrounded by market gardens and pastures until the nineteenth century. Cattle drovers coming from Kent to London markets such as Smithfield would stay at Peckham to graze their herds while they availed themselves of refreshment at the nearby aptly named public houses, The Red Cow or The Kentish Drovers.

Daniel Defoe (1660-1731), known chiefly as the author of *Robinson Crusoe* and *Moll Flanders* wrote more than 200

*Mural of Blake's vision – Goose Green, Peckham.
The poet is on the balcony on the left.*

other works, including *A Tour Through the Whole Island of Great Britain* in which he calls Peckham "a pleasant village"

By the end of the eighteenth century, as London developed and urbanisation spread into the surrounding countryside, Peckham was a village no more and "had many handsome houses... country seats of wealthy citizens of London".

The area developed a reputation for non-conformity: William Penn, the English Quaker and founder of Pennsylvania stayed at the Puritan Meeting House in Peckham and John Wesley, the evangelist and founder of Methodism, was a frequent visitor and preacher at the local Methodist Meeting. The Quaker reformer and businessman George Cadbury lived in one of the large houses that overlooked the Rye.

Besides non-conformity, Peckham became known for its educational establishments. There were at least four colleges or schools. The Irish playwright, Oliver Goldsmith, taught at Dr. Miller's Academy, even though he had such successes as the author of *She Stoops to Conquer* and *The Vicar of Wakefield*. He died a pauper and his friends had to contribute for a headstone for his grave. The poet Robert Browning attended the Reverend Thomas Reading's school in the High Street.

William Blake (1757-1827), the poet, engraver, painter and mystic, author of such pieces as *The Tiger* and Britain's second national anthem, *Jerusalem*, used to visit Peckham as a child of 9 years old, and he saw "a tree filled with angels, bright angelic wings bespangling every bough like stars". Unfortunately, when he returned home to Soho, his father, who was of a more prosaic temperament, beat him when told of young William's vision. It was only his mother's action that saved him from a worse thrashing. A month later he had a similar vision of angels approaching him as he walked across the Rye. Let's hope he didn't tell his dad that time.

Such spiritual experiences informed Blake's work as a poet and artist. Unfortunately, the public shared his father's attitude to his unique qualities. A leading critic called Blake "an unfortunate lunatic" and he sold little of his work. Since then his star has risen to the extent that on Sunday, September 18th, 2011, The Blake Society planted an "Angel Oak" near the spot where the young boy had his first vision. And even more colourfully, on the gable-end of a house at the junction of Hinkley Road and Ady's Road, is a mural commemorating Blake's mystical experience. It is well worth going to see.

The Rye was also the venue for a notorious fair which attracted all kinds of ne'er-do-wells and charlatans. It was one of the favourite haunts of Brockley Jack, a highwayman, one of the many villains who preyed on travellers in the area.

Transformation of the area continued with the arrival of the Grand Surrey Canal on which local market-garden produce was transported to the ever-encroaching capital and its hungry masses. Tilling's omnibus service from The Adam and Eve pub to the West End started in 1851. When the railways finally arrived in 1865 opportunistic builders followed. They began to throw up houses on open fields and cast greedy eyes on Rye Common. Such was the alarm that the Vestry, in 1868, bought the 64 acres of the Common to save it from development and in 1890 also bought 49 acres of Homestall farm to create Peckham Rye Park. This means that in one of the most heavily built-up and populous areas of south-east London there are 113 acres of open space and greenery that people can use for recreation.

The battle for the Common was not the only or most famous battle on the Rye for legend has it that Boudicca (Boadicea), Queen of the Iceni, (whose name is derived from the Celtic word for victory), fought here with the Romans in AD 60. Before her husband, Prasutagus, died the Iceni had lived in some harmony with the invading Romans, so much so that the King had named the Emperor Nero as his heir, along with his wife and two daughters, perhaps hoping that by doing so the Romans would be content with their share and at least some property would pass to his family. However, the Roman Procurator (governor) wanted more and when Boudicca refused, she was stripped and flogged and her two daughters were raped in front of her. The Romans made the mistake of leaving the Queen alive, no doubt thinking that a woman would cause them no bother. They had another think coming.

Boudicca rallied her subjects, made alliances with other tribes and began her bloody revenge by advancing on Colchester, a town of 120,000 people, and razing it to the ground. She went on to destroy London and St. Albans before the Roman Governor, Suetonius Paulinas, who was in North Wales subduing the Druids and chopping down their sacred groves of oak trees on Anglesey, heard of it. He raced south and local legend claims that battle took place between the Romans and Britons on the Rye. Tacitus, the Roman historian, wrote that 80,000 Celts died and only 400 Romans. Whether this is merely propaganda or not, it is known that the defeated Boudicca, rather than be taken prisoner and possibly exhibited in triumph in Rome, killed herself, some say by taking poison. She is said to be buried beneath what is now Platform 10 on King's Cross Station but her bronze statue by Thomas Thorneycroft, facing the Houses of Parliament on the north end of Westminster Bridge, carries on its plinth the inscription from William Cowper's *Boudicca: An Ode*

> Regions Caesar never knew
> Thy posterity shall sway.

All this is a far cry from the modern, multicultural south London suburb of today but when wandering down Rye Lane amid the vibrant street life and the stalls of exotic fare, it's worth remembering Boudicca who took on the might of Rome and almost won: not bad for an Essex girl.

Palimpsest

"Palimpsest?" Me neither. I had to look it up in Chambers Dictionary where it says "a manuscript in which old writing has been rubbed out to make room for new: a monumental brass turned over for a new inscription". Having done that, I understood what the lecturer had meant when he said, "The City of London is a palimpsest". And he was so right, for the Square Mile of the UK's capital city is constantly changing; old buildings being demolished to make way for more modern (and lucrative) ones. 'Twas ever so. Layer upon layer of history lies beneath our feet, from Roman through all the ages and dynasties to the second Elizabethan. A good example of this is Wallbrook, which runs between Cannon Street and Victoria Street, debouching into that area besides the Mansion House where five of the main City thoroughfares meet.

Like the Effra, the Neckinger, the Bourne, the Black Ditch and many others, the Walbrook is one of London's so-called "lost rivers". It is claimed that it gets its name from the fact that it ran alongside the old Roman wall to the north of the City before entering it and flowing through what is now a busy financial centre to enter the Thames somewhere not far east of another lost river – The Fleet – which, culverted now, comes out under the north bank of Blackfriars' Bridge. Others claim that its name is derived from the Old English *Wealas,* the stream "of the Britons". Whatever the case may be, you can't see the Walbrook now but what was found buried in its bed in 1954 gave rise to much excitement amongst scholars and the public alike with over 80,000 visitors eager to see it.

At first, when Professor W. F. Grimes, the then Director of the Museum of London and his team of archaeologists uncovered the remains, it was thought to be an early Christian church but it proved to be a temple, a Mithraeum, built in the mid-third century and dedicated to Mithras, the Persian god of the Sun and Heavenly Light. Its almost subterranean position represented the cave in which Mithras slew the primordial bull, thereby letting the powers of Life and Creativity into the world. This slaying of the bull, the Tauroctony, was on a marble relief found in the temple. Other reliefs of Minerva, Mercury, and Venus were found in the ruins, but Mithras is the chief deity of the religion which was secret and open only to men who rose through its various levels by initiation. It extolled the virtues of courage and integrity which helps explain why it was popular among Roman soldiers and traders who must have brought it to Britain.

Mithraism held communal services with followers sitting on benches either side of a narrow nave, which led to an altar. Shared meals of bread and wine were common. It laid especial emphasis on a saviour (Mithras), sacrifice, and rebirth with a festival on or near the Winter Solstice, 25th December, the darkest day before the coming again of Sol Invictus, the Unconquerable Sun. Sounds a bit like another syncretic religion from the Middle East – Christianity.

The Mithras Temple, Wallbrook

Another example of borrowing can be found in the form of the Mithraeum. Besides its liturgical similarities, the temple may have been a forerunner of the now very familiar shape of Christian churches: there were aisles flanking a long nave leading to an altar and there was an apse.

When it was first built, the temple stood on the east bank of the Walbrook, now lost beneath the busy City above. Due to building needs, it was later moved to Temple Court in Queen Victoria Street and is displayed on an elevated position so that the public can view it, even though it was turned 90 degrees to face north. The marble heads of Mithras, Serapis, and Minerva, the statuette of Mercury and other sculptures and inscriptions were transferred to the Museum of London where they are displayed.

The Temple of Mithras was discovered because a huge office block was to be built there. Bucklersbury House was the first London building to break through the height limit of 100ft, which had been the convention for centuries. It was a

The Tauroctony, slaying of the Bull, by Mitraus. This fresco is nearby.

daring innovation, an attempt by the City Fathers to introduce a new commercial style and the maximum square footage of office space. It might well have succeeded but at what price? The 14-storey slab was called "the largest and dullest of London's 1950's office blocks" by Sir Nikolaus Pevsner, the architectural historian, in his *Guide to the City of London*. And now, ironically, the block has been demolished and there are plans to remove the Temple of Mithras to its original site on the east bank of the hidden Wallbrook. No Bull. The City of London is a palimpsest indeed. If you don't believe me, count the cranes.

Carry On, Whitehall

A metonym is a literary device whereby a detail is made to represent a whole e. g. "the press" for newspapers and journalists; "the stage" for theatres and actors; "the Bench" for courts, judges etc. "Whitehall" is the metonym which has come to represent Government offices, departments of state, and those employed therein, (though there are those who have more "colourful" names for those Faceless Ones who run/ruin our lives).

Many are unaware that this grand thoroughfare, which runs for just over half a mile, is actually two streets – Whitehall at the northern end near Trafalgar Square and at the southern end, beyond the Cenotaph, it becomes Parliament Street. At one time, part of it was named York Place after the London home of Cardinal Wolsey, Archbishop of York and Henry VIII's chief adviser, until that son of an Ipswich butcher fell foul of his Royal master and Henry took over the episcopal palace and changed the name to Whitehall. It became a main artery in the capital, a centre of Royal power, and has remained synonymous with the administration of the kingdom ever since.

The sprawling Palace which once occupied the area was burnt down in 1698 and all that remains of it is Inigo Jones'

In Craig's Court is Harrington House. It was the last private house in Whitehall up until the 1st World War. It is now part of a telephone exchange.

classical masterpiece, the Banqueting House of 1622 from one window of which the unfortunate monarch, King Charles I, stepped to his beheading and martyrdom and, at the back of the Ministry of Defence, Queen Mary's Steps, by which the Catholic monarch, daughter of Catharine of Aragon and King Henry VIII, gained access to the Tudor palace when approaching by Royal Barge on the Thames. Her father's wine cellar also lies beneath the Ministry of Defence (used for receptions today) and across the main road, beneath Cockpit Passage are the remnants of where the much married King played Real Tennis. I wonder if all his opponents let him win. Worth it to keep your head.

Along this broad avenue can be found, among other important offices, the Admiralty, the War Office, Horse Guards, Gwydyr House (the Welsh Office), the Foreign and Commonwealth Office and, in an adjoining side street, 10 Downing Street, the official residence of Her Majesty the

Queen's Prime Minister and First Lord of the Treasury. It was not always so for at one time many grand private houses lined the street. Dover House, up near the northern end, which now houses the Scottish Office, was once Melbourne House and home to one of the most influential political salons of the nineteenth century where Lady Melbourne held court for the Whig Party. It was here that one of the great scandals of the time dominated the news.

William Lamb, MP for Leominster, was Lady Melbourne's son and had a distinguished career ahead of him, but there was a fly in the political ointment in the shape of his headstrong, flighty young wife, Caroline, who had been only nineteen at their marriage. They moved into the upper part of Melbourne House (the lower part being the domain of Lord and Lady Melbourne), which was a centre of society where grand balls were held and the doors were open to the rich, powerful, famous and interesting. It was to one of these occasions that George Gordon, Lord Byron, who fulfilled at least the last two categories, came and the scene was set for a love affair that shocked decent society (even in an age when many marriages accommodated a certain degree of laissez-faire where matters of the heart were concerned).

Byron had become an overnight sensation with the publication of *Childe Harold's Pilgrimage*, a poetic tale of doomed youth. Everyone wanted to meet him, to have him as a guest at their party. Lady Melbourne must have regretted the presence of this young man who had a club-foot and who bit his nails down to the quick, at her ball for her young daughter-in-law began a four month liaison with the poet that shamed even that aged lady who "had climbed the social ladder on her back" and had as two of her lovers, George, Prince of Wales and his brother, the Duke of York. She had many illegitimate children which her long-suffering husband adopted as his own. Talk about the pot calling the kettle black.

No doubt there was some reason for concern for Caro, as she was known, was less than stable at times. She was given to cross-dressing and had even managed to disguise herself as a man to attend the maiden speech of her husband in Parliament where women were not allowed. She shocked society in other ways also, for example, while it was common for lovers to exchange locks of hair which were kept as tokens of affection, Caroline sent Byron some of her pubic hair with a graphic note attached to it. It may have been desperation on her part because after four torrid months the affair was burnt out as far as the poet was concerned, but Caroline pursued him ruthlessly. She was thought to be on the verge of madness and Byron turned to her mother-in law for help, who was more than accommodating according to the gossip of the time. She also arranged a meeting with her niece, Annabella Milbanke, and when this progressed to an impending marriage, Caro slashed herself with a knife in public and made a scene at a triumphal ball given for the Duke of Wellington. Too, too much.

Lady Melbourne's son, William Lamb, became one of Queen Victoria's favourite Prime Ministers, and was given the title Lord Melbourne. He remained a constant husband to his wayward wife. Byron's marriage to Annabella was a failure and his behaviour became so scandalous that he fled

The Scotland Office at Dover House, once Melbourne House where Lady Caroline Lamb and Lord Byron's paths crossed with scandalous results

abroad where he became a Greek national hero when he died at Missolonghi in the War of Independence from the Turks. Caroline Lamb died young at forty-two in 1828. And much of the drama of this famous affair went on behind the doors of what is now Dover House. The bedroom where she and Byron sported is now an office and in the grand entrance hall on the left of the staircase is a poignant reminder of this nineteenth century scandal, "Byron's Rope" which was placed there to assist the club-footed poet up the stairs because on his first entry he had stumbled into the life of Caroline Lamb and become, as she claimed, "mad, bad and dangerous to know", words which some claim could be applied to her as well. So, as you can see, it has not always been pen-pushing behind the doors of Whitehall.

This can be further illustrated by a tale of happenings with a flavour of farce across the road from Dover House in a little-noticed alley that leads to Craig's Court, a place that deserves more recognition (and public thanks) for the part it played in the development of London's urban landscape.

Can you imagine what life would be like without pavements, if pedestrians were not separated from vehicular traffic? It's bad enough trying to make your way along the congested walkways of urban areas in most places, but in London it can be a struggle of Homeric proportions. Have you ever tried to manoeuvre along Oxford Street at sales time? Or tried to cross the road at Parliament Square amid the throngs of visitors eager to see the sights? It's hell, but without pavements it would be even worse. And for pavements we have an incident in Craig's Court to thank.

Eighteenth century London was a messy and dangerous place for those on foot. The streets were not only so dirty that ladies often had to wear pattens, wooden overshoes which raised their fine dresses above the mud and filth underfoot, but because there was no differentiation between walkers, coaches, and all other wheeled traffic that filled the streets, you took your life in your hands when you went out on foot – crossing the road could be suicidal. No wonder crossing-sweepers were necessary.

In Craig's Court is the handsome Harrington House, once home of the eponymous Earl but now a telephone exchange. It was built in 1702 by the then Earl who hoped that proximity to the new Whitehall palace (which he thought was going to be built almost next door) would mean advancement for himself and his offspring. Disappointment followed because the Tudor palace was never rebuilt and Harrington House was no longer near the centre of power as desired. The family stayed there until it became the last private house in Whitehall with a narrow alleyway as its connection to the main thoroughfare. They did not up sticks until the First World War, in 1917.

It was the alleyway that was instrumental in gaining pavements for the capital, for in 1762 the Pavement Bill was put forward in the House of Commons. Heated debate followed as to who was to pay for this improvement, the householders or the general public by way of tax? The matter was settled when Speaker Onslow came in his coach to visit the Earl of Harrington. Unfortunately, the coach was too wide and became stuck in the narrow passageway and the Speaker of the House of Commons, an exalted position, had to be pulled out through a hole cut in the roof of his carriage. Sounds like something from a panto or a silent film doesn't it? Anyway, Onslow stormed off back to the House and gave his casting vote in favour of householders providing pavements outside their homes. Thank goodness for that.

So, while most people think of Whitehall as full of offices of state or as a grand processional route for such occasions as Remembrance Day at the Cenotaph, it does have a less-serious side to its history.

Absolutely Fabulous in Cheam

The provocative English author, G. K. Chesterton (1874-1936), wrote that "Surrey is the debatable land between London and England. It is not a county but a border; it is there that South London meets and makes war on Sussex". One of the places where you can see reminders of this war is Cheam in the London Borough of Sutton, the capital's smallest borough, which is a combination of city and country. Despite lying within a few miles of the centre of London, it has more than 1,000 acres of open spaces and many reminders of its history remain.

Perhaps the most famous resident and one remembered by my fellow wrinklies, was Anthony Aloysius St. John Hancock, star of the 50's and 60's radio and television series *Hancock's Half Hour* who lived at the fictional 23 Railway Cuttings, East Cheam. But it was the very real King Henry VIII who put the area on the map.

Although appearing in William the Conqueror's Magna Carta, his great inventory of who owned what and how much it was worth, when "Ceiham" had one church, 17 ploughs and woodland worth 17 hogs, it was the second Tudor king, Henry VIII, who brought fame to Cheam. In 1538 he bought land there, destroyed a village and church and built Nonsuch

Palace, a magnificent residence of the finest materials to reflect the monarch's power and wealth. Unfortunately, Henry died before it was completed and the palace passed down to various Royals until King Charles II gave it to his doxy, Lady Castlemaine, who had it pulled down and sold off in order to pay her gambling debts. A Gothic revival mansion in Nonsuch Park is all that remains to remind us of previous glories.

In the centre of the village is Whitehall, a splendid timber-framed and weatherboarded house, built about 1500. It has seen a number of uses, starting as a yeoman farmer's house and graduating to one of the sites in the village that housed Cheam Preparatory School, (attended by H. R. H. The Duke of Edinburgh, before it moved to new premises in Berkshire where his son, H. R. H, The Prince of Wales attended). The space is now filled with exhibits that tell the history of the area.

It is across The Broadway from Whitehall on the other side of the road that we find what is considered to be Cheam's greatest treasure and one that is not widely known or visited. In the churchyard of St. Dunstan's and forming part of the Cheam Conservation area is the Lumley Chapel, a redundant Anglican church designated as Grade II Listed by English Heritage and under the care of the Churches Conservation Trust.

The Lumley Chapel has been called "the Westminster Abbey of the suburbs", not for the magnificence of its architecture but for its contents. The original church, dedicated to St. Dunstan, was founded by the Archbishop of Canterbury early in the eleventh century. Over the years it was altered and, eventually, demolished with the exception of the Chapel, which was the chancel of the parish church, and a new one was built nearby. The Lumley Chapel is the oldest building in the Borough with Saxon and Norman fragments. It stands in the churchyard amid gravestones and yew trees and its simple structure of roughcast rubble, stone and brick belies the richness to be found within.

In 1580 the first Baron Lumley married well and part of the dowry of his wife, Jane Fitzalan, daughter of the Earl of Arundel, was Nonsuch Palace. In the 1590's Lumley began to alter the church, making it into a memorial chapel for himself and his two wives. He was a cultured man, possessing a famous collection of paintings and books, many of which were kept at his main dwelling, Lumley Castle in County Durham. The books were later bought by the first Stuart king of England, James I, and formed the nucleus of the Royal Library, which in turn became the basis of the British Library.

Lord Lumley had the walls of the Chapel plastered and along the top of two walls is a very attractive frieze of foliage and fruit. Above is a plastered barrel-vaulted roof decorated with ribs and pendentives on one of which is the date 1592. But it is the tombs and memorials that give the place its splendour. That of his first wife, Jane, is made of alabaster with marble pilasters and rich heraldic details. The panels show Jane and her children kneeling in prayer. Opposite is the tomb of Elizabeth Darcy, his second wife. This too is of finely carved marble and alabaster.

Lord Lumley's own tomb stands next to Elizabeth's. Once again, it too is of alabaster and marble and is heavily decorated

The Lumley Chapel, Cheam

with heraldic devices. It has the Lumley family motto on it "*Murus Aenus Sana Conscientia*" (a sound conscience is a wall of brass). It is historically interesting but lacks the touch of the personal that his wives' tombs have.

As though these three tombs were not enough for the limited space of the Chapel, there are many others also. A local family, the Pybuses of Cheam House, are well represented, as are the Antrobuses of Lower Cheam House. There is a memorial to Edmund Barrett who was Serjeant of the Wine Cellar to the ill-fated King Charles I. A touching memorial records the death of five-year-old Ann Gilpin, daughter of the Headmaster of Cheam School. Brasses from the original church are there, too. It is rare for so many funerary monuments, and such splendid ones, to be found in so small a repository but they make the Lumley Chapel "absolutely fabulous" and, yes, Joanna is a descendant.

The Harvest of the Sea

Lower Thames Street in the City of London has little to recommend it. Dotted with speed-cameras, it is merely functional: a fast but usually traffic-jammed dual carriageway used to avoid the central roads of the Square Mile. One authority calls the A3211 "a dank and unwelcoming place to be". At one time it was known as one street, Thames Street, but is now divided into Upper and Lower sections at the London Bridge underpass, in neither of which does the pedestrian wish to linger.

The Lower Thames Street section has cut off those buildings on the waterfront of the Thames overlooking the Pool of London from that historic and interesting northward sloping area of small alleys and passageways stretching up to Eastcheap which are worth exploring, and has left a sliver of land on which are some buildings of note. There is Wren's church of St. Magnus the Martyr, called an "inexplicable splendour of Ionian white and gold" by T. S. Eliot; Robert Smirke's Custom House with its impressive riverfront facade; and, most attractive in a French Renaissance style, best seen from the south bank of the river, the old Billingsgate Fish Market with its golden fish weather vane, which closed in January 1982 when its function as a market for piscine products was moved east to the Isle of Dogs.

The old Billingsgate Fish Market

Although its chief raison d'être has been moved not all links with its piscine past have gone from the area. The Fishmongers' Company, the fourth of the Twelve Great Livery Companies in the City, has its Hall nearby, at the north-west corner of London Bridge and the Watermen have their Hall in one of those little streets that make the area so interesting and nearby is, Saint-Mary-at-Hill. Which brings us to the main subject of this account?

London has many attractions both for the foreign visitor and the home-grown one. Among them are its old customs and ceremonies such as The Trooping of the Colour in June, The Remembrance Sunday Ceremony and The Lord Mayor's Show both in November, but there are less famous customs of which many are ignorant, such as The Blessing of the Throats at St. Etheldreda's Church in February, the Ceremony of the Knollys Rose in June and the Harvest of the Sea at the church of St. Mary at Hill in the first half of October.

John Betjeman described St. Mary's as "the least spoiled and most gorgeous interior in the City". One of the least damaged churches by the Great Fire of 1666, it was one of the first to be restored by Sir Christopher Wren between 1670 and 1676 at a cost of £3,980. When you consider its position among the narrow lanes which include Fish Street Hill and Pudding Lane, and its nearness to "the great fish depot of the Metropolis", it comes as no surprise to discover its associations with the fishing industry even though that has now moved away downriver. Nathaniel Hawthorne wrote of the area in 1857 as being "a dirty, evil-smelling, crowded precinct thronged with people carrying fish on their heads" and full of "rough men and slatternly women". The word "Billingsgate" was synonymous with foulness and crudery. Obviously there was a need for a Christian presence which St. Mary's has provided throughout the centuries and still does, but it can be a little difficult to find one's way in. The rear of the church in a lane of the same name, St.-Mary-at-Hill, is the grander of the two approaches, being classical and imposing, but the entry in Lovat Lane is simpler and less obvious to find (though you could try the rear passageway if you are not put off by the skull and crossbones that stare down at you).

I managed to find the entrance on October 9th, 2011, my nose having been led by the strong smell of fish. The door was open and the white-coated fishmongers, everyone a gent, welcomed me even though I was an hour early for the Harvest of the Sea. They were busy arranging a magnificent display of many types of seafood from shellfish to octopus, from dabs to Dover sole, on a large slab in the vestibule of the church. All was artfully displayed and backed by fishing nets and lifebuoys. Some of the fishmongers wore their traditional straw boaters but one of them, well into his eighties, proudly showed me his very heavy, leather, flat-topped hat that he wore when he carried the baskets of fish on his head. He told me that the design of the hat had evolved from those worn by King Henry V's bowmen at the Battle of Agincourt. He was proud of that, and rightly so.

Although the church no longer has its box pews, it is certainly a magnificent space. The vaulted roof that came down in a fire in 1988 has been restored to its original splendour, as has most of the rest of the building. It is most suitable not only for worship but for the theatricality of the Harvest of the Sea, for members of the Billingsgate Ward, officials from associated guilds and churchmen, all dressed in their fine robes, process from beneath the famous William Hill organ, (built in 1848 and one of the most important in the UK) to the accompaniment of one of the foremost a cappella groups. The long and distinguished musical tradition of the church is kept up and Thomas Tallis, a sixteenth century music maker at St. Mary's would be proud of it.

The service began and as one would expect – all the prayers, readings and hymns had a nautical theme: we had an introit by Thomas Campion suitably entitled *Never Weather-Beaten Saile*, the hymns *Lead Us Heavenly Father lead Us O'er the World's Tempestuous Sea* and *Eternal Father, Strong to Save Whose Arm Hath Bound the Restless Wave*, the anthem *Sunset and Evening Star* and, to end, *The National Anthem*. All were sung with gusto. There was even a special *Billingsgate Market Prayer* written by a past Dean of York.

The porter on the left is wearing the traditional heavy flat-topped leather hat on which baskets of fish were balanced. Tradition claims that this design evolved from the hats worn by the bowmen at the Battle of Agincourt in 1415

And what of the fish? I hear you ask. In keeping with tradition, they were donated to charitable causes. I'm not sure I should be telling you this in case you turn up and eat all the grub, but I've left the best for last, for laid out on trestle tables was a most splendid buffet and we all tucked in at the end. Can't wait for next year!

The One-Way Ticket Railway

On Wednesday, September 5th, 1979, Admiral of The Fleet, the Earl Mountbatten of Burma, murdered by the IRA nine days earlier, was given a State funeral at the end of which the cortege bore the coffin, draped with the Union flag, to Waterloo Station for the final journey to the family home, Romsey Abbey, in Hampshire, and in doing so added another extraordinary chapter to this remarkable man's life.

The dead, like "taxes and the poor, are always with us" in one form or another and accommodating them has been a problem throughout the ages, whether they are fed to the vultures on the Towers of Silence or burned on pyres on the banks of the Ganges. The Victorians, ever resourceful, thought up a number of ways to solve the problem created by the deceased of the growing industrial cities, especially the capital. Edwin Chadwick, the social reformer, planned to build a huge new cemetery at Abbey Wood to which corpses were to be brought by steamboats specially built for the purpose. It was reckoned that at least a hundred bodies would be brought each day to the impressive (at least on paper) tree-lined grounds beside the Thames in SE2. Unfortunately or not, the relevant health authorities thought the river would be further polluted and the scheme floundered. Another scheme was to build a gigantic pyramid on Primrose Hill that would hold in its 94 floors five million bodies. Can you imagine such a blot on the landscape? Thank goodness it never got off the ground.

However, there was one novel plan that did see the light of day. The London Necropolis and National Mausoleum Company was created by Act of Parliament in 1852. The Company bought 500 acres of land from the Earl of Onslow at Brookwood, near Woking in Surrey, to create what was at one time the largest cemetery in the world. It was so large that it was estimated that it would meet London's needs for the next 500 years.

In 1854 the Brookwood Cemetery, a massive metropolitan burial ground, was opened. The Necropolis Railway, a private railway run by the London and South Western Railway Co., solved the problem of how to get the dear departed to Surrey from the capital by transporting coffins and mourners straight to the cemetery. It was a success and a specially constructed platform was built at Waterloo to meet its needs. Apparently, there were two ticket machines, one for the living that issued return tickets and another that issued one-way tickets for the coffins. Is it any wonder the train was given such irreverent names as *The Stiffs' Express* or *The One-Way Train*?

When Waterloo was reconstructed in the early nineteenth century, this platform was demolished and a replacement one was built at 121 Westminster Bridge Road. This too continued to fill a popular need and the special trains carrying the deceased and their mourning families left south London a dozen times a day in its busiest period, though as the years passed and alternative burial grounds were established, this

This is what remains of the "One-Ticket Railway"

decreased to one a day which left at 11:00 a. m. , giving the mourners time to go to the funeral and get back in time for dinner.

The scheme was not without its critics. Class distinction raised its ugly head even in death and there were those, including the Bishop of London, who worried that ne'er-do-wells might be placed in proximity to more respectable folk. So much for Christian charity and death being a leveller. Do you think the contents of the coffins cared?

Such "pressing" problems were solved in the usual British way, by segregation. The Upper Crust was placed in First-Class compartments with all the trimmings that such accommodation affords. Those mere mortals who could not aspire to such luxury were given Third-Class treatment. Did they honestly think that St. Peter waited at the Pearly Gates at the end of the line, clipping the tickets and charging excess for those who had been placed in the wrong class, or telling them to wait their turn? What tosh!

There were further divisions at the cemetery where separate trains went into separate stations. Those who adhered to the Church of England went to the South Station, which was claimed to be cold and damp because it was lower lying, and those who were Nonconformists went to the sunnier uplands of the Northern Station. Once again, do you think the departed (who were by now enjoying the delights of the Elysian Fields) gave a hoot, that's if they'd had the right ticket and had got past St. Peter?

By the mid-1930's the demand for the services of the Necropolis had fallen along with the revenue. The Second World War gave it its final blow. It was bombed by the Germans on April 14th, 1941, and was never replaced. However, there is one reminder of it. At one time, in a vain attempt to prevent hardening of the arteries and to keep my errant mind in trim, I used to attend classes at Morley College, that excellent institution established by Emma Cons and which was originally housed in The Old Vic. As I walked down Lower Marsh I sometimes wondered what that building was across the road, adorned with marble pillars and lions heads. It looked so incongruous on that short uninspiring stretch of Westminster Road. On investigation, it proved to be the old entrance to the Necropolis Railway, which was no longer used, except for one last occasion when the line was reopened on Wednesday September 5th, 1979, for the funeral train that took the last Viceroy of India to his resting place in the Hampshire countryside.

From Bootleg Bibles to Bedpans

There used to be on the wall of the building where Cornhill curves round into Lombard Street in the City of London, a plaque that said something to the effect that "Thomas Guy, Bookseller, had his shop here". It's been gone for a good few years now, goodness knows why, but it was another little piece of the capital's history that has disappeared. I wonder if most people who noticed it realised that it commemorated the founder of one of London's great teaching hospitals. Although founded in 1723, Guy's was one of the new hospitals, St Bartholomew's having been founded in 1123, St. Thomas's in 1173, and Westminster in 1720.

But what of Sir Thomas Guy (1644-1724) and how did he make so large a fortune that he could found a hospital? There were various sources, some of which caused one critic to write in the *Gentleman's Magazine* of November 1754 that Guy "had amassed prodigious fortune, not indeed with great honour to himself or good to the community".

The son of a coal monger and lighterman (whose job it was to carry goods across from larger ships to shore in a small boat), Guy was born in Horselydown, a poor area of London on the south side of the River Thames, near where Tower Bridge now stands. He was eight when his father died and his

A plaque commemorating Thomas Guy's birthplace

mother took Guy and his siblings to her home town of Tamworth to bring them up.

When he was sixteen he was apprenticed to a bookseller in Cheapside and it was in this trade that Thomas laid down the foundations of what was to become one of the sources of his great wealth.

In 1668, after completing his apprenticeship, Guy became a member of the Stationers' Company and set up in business as a bookseller. He saw an opening in the market that he could profitably fill. The printing of Bibles, which were expensive and usually printed on poor quality paper, was a monopoly held by Oxford University Press, the Stationers' Company, and the King's Printers. Guy illegally imported Bibles of better quality from Holland and undercut those available by the usual means. His riches began to grow as he sold better quality Bibles that everyone could afford. He was so successful that eventually he went into business with Oxford University itself, thereby setting the seal on his reputation and ensuring a continuation of his wealth.

Another source of income was the buying of seamens' tickets. Sailors were not paid in cash but given tickets that they had to redeem for cash at the Naval Office in London when they returned from tours of duty. Guy bought these at a cheaper rate from the ever-needy sailors and redeemed that at a higher rate. Many thought this a questionable practice and it added to the rumours that he was a miser who ate his dinner on his shop counter off any old newspaper he could find.

But the main source of his prosperity was the South Sea Company, which had been given the monopoly to trade with Spanish South American colonies in return for assuming the national debt which England had incurred during the War of Spanish Succession. Additionally, it was given the right to transport slaves from West Africa to North America and during its operations it shipped over 30,000 slaves across the Atlantic.

Such a business, talked up by its directors and by rumours which flourished about the fortunes to be made meant that there was great speculation from all walks of life and over the course of one twelve month period the price of stock went from about £100 a share to nearly £1,000. It was too good to last, but before the Bubble burst Guy (who held £45,000 worth of stock) sold his holdings and made an immense fortune.

It was not only his wealth that prospered. Guy also ascended the greasy pole of politics and in 1695 became MP for Tamworth, his home town. It was here that his philanthropic instinct first showed itself. He donated money for the building and maintenance of almshouses. He also had built a splendid new Town Hall which he threatened to have torn down when

The tomb of Thomas Guy in the chapel of the hospital he founded

he was rejected as the MP in 1707. He was obviously a man with strong feelings, especially when those feelings were crossed. This can be seen in incident involving money and specific directions.

Guy was a bachelor and his friends, thinking that marriage might do him good, persuaded him to propose marriage to his housekeeper, Phyllis. He did so and the engagement was announced but, one day when the master was out, poor Phyllis made the mistake of allowing the workmen who were laying pavement outside his shop to exceed the boundary by a mere six inches, something that would cost Guy more. He was not pleased and broke off the engagement. It seems that Guy was one of those people who will strain at a gnat but swallow a camel for, having become a Governor of St. Thomas's Hospital, he gave £1,000 for three new wards.

Sir Thomas Guy was a complex character: he had a fortune yet dressed shabbily, so much so that once, so the story goes, as he stood on the bridge staring at the river and lost in thought, a passer-by took him for a down-and-out contemplating suicide and thrust a sovereign into his grubby hand. Guy was touched by this and caught the man up, said who he was and returned the gold coin. Sometime later, he heard that his would-be benefactor had gone bankrupt and Guy rescued him and his business.

The position of Sheriff of the City of London was a great honour, one that was bestowed only on those who were thought worthy of it, but when Guy was offered the title he refused and paid the fine of £400 which was a great deal less than the expense of being Sheriff would have cost him with all the staff and elaborate entertaining that would have been expected.

As a Governor of St. Thomas's, he came into contact with some of the staff on a regular basis and one of them, Dr. Mead, mindful of Guy's wealth, his single status, and the fact that he had already given so much to one hospital, suggested that he found another, "for incurables, nearby" and the foundations of Guy's hospital was begun across the road in the spring of 1722. Guy visited the site regularly but, while most of it was finished, he died on Boxing Day 1724 before it was completed.

A strange man, a mixture of the mean and the generous, we are lucky to benefit from the latter of those traits in the shape of one of the great teaching hospitals of London, Guy's Hospital.

Heads and Tales

Never let it be said that the Faceless Ones who subtly create and control our surroundings don't have a sense of irony.

I remember one Saturday morning walking past Westminster Hall when I was stopped by one of the many tourists thronging the pavement. He wanted me to take his photo standing with Hamo Thorneycroft's bronze statue of Oliver Cromwell in the background. I did so. We got talking and he turned out to be Vietnamese and a Professor of French Literature at one the universities in the Francophone Maghreb. When he learned that I taught English Literature, he put his arm around my shoulder – with some difficulty for some South-East Asians are even shorter than us South Walians – and asked another passer-by to take a photograph of us. I suggested we ought to have our picture taken across the road beneath the bust of King Charles I in a niche on the back of St. Margaret's church. This we duly did and then we moved to the Victoria Tower Gardens on the south side of the Houses of Parliament (everybody has seen these on TV but few know their name. It's where they have all those boring interviews with MP's). There we sat and chatted for an hour or so.

I asked him why he had chosen Cromwell to be commemorated with. He turned out to be of that party that saw the Member of Parliament for Huntingdon in 1628 as a hero of liberty rather than a regicidal dictator. He asked me why I had chosen to be pictured with the King Cromwell had executed. "In the interests of historical fairness," I airily said. A good-natured argument ensued until we broke for ice-lollies, sat and watched the Thames flow past and then, Mivvies finished, went our separate ways. I had always wondered who had placed the lead bust of the beheaded Stuart in such a position, facing his nemesis, but I was glad it had been so for it not only gave me a pleasant interlude with an engaging stranger but it made me want to find out more about the two sculptures.

Britain's only military dictator has long been the subject of controversy. Was he a regicidal tyrant who, had he lived longer, would have made himself monarch, but why should he bother with such a trifle when he was king in all but name, having accepted the title of Lord Protector? Or was he the guardian of our civil liberties against the indulgent and flaccid Stuart dynasty who thought they were God's anointed representatives on Earth? The controversy even enveloped the statue of which we speak.

It is said that "Politics is the art of the possible". Nowhere is this more obvious than in 1895, when the Liberal government of Lord Roseberry had a small majority and was dependant upon the support of the Irish Members of Parliament for their continuance in power. When Roseberry, who admired Cromwell, proposed a statue of the Lord Protector be erected outside the House of Commons, the Irish members who remembered the cruelty of Cromwell's rule in Ireland, especially the massacre

The statue of Oliver Cromwell, outside Parliament, (left) ironically looks across at the bust of King Charles I (right), at the back of St. Margaret's, the King to whose death Cromwell was one of the signatories.

at Drogheda, all voted against it. Roseberry's Bill was defeated, an election was held and the Tories won.

However, some few years later, the plan for a statue was successfully revived. Some say that it only received consent because it was to be placed in that piece of land known as "the Pit" (as it is below the level of the road) and this gave some satisfaction to the Irish MP's who claimed that was where Cromwell deserved to be. Today he watches over the comings and goings of Parliament from the Pit. Strangely, an anonymous donor gave the £500 pounds necessary to get the project started. Everyone suspected that it was Roseberry himself who gave the money.

While this explained to me the origins of Cromwell's statue, it did not satisfy my curiosity about the bust of King Charles I, which stares across the traffic at his chief executioner. I wrote to the Library at Westminster Abbey which keeps the records for St. Margaret's church and had a very prompt reply from the Assistant Keeper of the Muniments who wrote:

> "The lead bust was discovered, with another which is now at the Banqueting House in Whitehall, in an antique shop in London by a member of The Society of King Charles the Martyr. It was presented to St Margaret's in 1950 but not erected until 1956, as a new niche had to be made for it. It is thought to be late eighteenth century or earlier and copied from the Van Dyck portrait of the King. The sculptor is unknown, or neither is where it originated."

But there is more to the story.

After the Restoration of the monarchy in 1660, when the Stuart Line regained the throne, Charles II had Cromwell posthumously attainted for high treason and his body disinterred from Westminster Abbey where The Lord Protector had been laid to rest among the tombs of kings and queens. His head was then put on a spike outside Westminster Hall for about twenty years. It is now in Sidney Sussex College, Cambridge. His name, however, has resonated down the ages and incurred displeasure in certain quarters.

In 1875 a statue of Cromwell was placed outside Manchester Cathedral, which was seen as an insensitive move by the large Irish population of the city. They weren't the only ones. When Queen Victoria was invited to open the new Town Hall, she consented on the condition that the statue be removed. The

Council refused, the statue stayed and Victoria declined to open the Town Hall. The statue was later relocated outside Wythenshawe Hall.

Before the First World War, when he was First Lord of the Admiralty, Winston Churchill suggested naming a battleship *H.M.S. Cromwell*. The suggestion did not receive royal approval. During the Second World War "Cromwell" was the code word warning that German invasion was imminent.

Martyr King and his Executioner remain locked in each other's gaze across the road and through the ages. Irony, indeed.

Cheaper by the Cartload

I doubt if the shoppers who fill Oxford Street or those of the bon ton who once lived in the grand houses on Park Lane would know that the former was once named Tyburn Road and the latter Tyburn Lane. They were originally named after the stream that rose in Hampstead, made its way towards Regents Park, across Picadilly, under Buckingham Palace and then onwards to the Thames and from 1388-1783 was one of the chief places of execution in the capital. Indeed, it is thought that the many elm trees that originally lined the banks of the Tyburn were, before the introduction of a gallows, convenient for hanging those who fell foul of the many laws that still had death as a penalty. Such grisly associations might have put them off shopping or living there and that is why, in 1782, the names were changed. Now where Tyburn Tree once stood with its crop of strange fruit stands Marble Arch, one of London's busiest junctions. The Arch, which was originally intended as an imposing entry to Buckingham Palace in 1827 as part of George IV's grandiose plans for London, proved to be too narrow for the Royal coaches and in 1851, the year of the Great Exhibition, was moved to its present position. Only members of the Royal Family are allowed to drive through it.

On the wall of Tyburn Convent is this plaque to Catholic Martyrs

Another reason for Tyburn becoming a place of execution was that at the start of its notorious history (beginning with the execution of Nicholas Bembre on February 20th, 1388, who was hanged for treason) it was open fields and therefore suited the philosophy of hanging as a deterrent: folk could come to see the fate of malefactors and, so the idea went, be put off following a similar lifestyle with its inevitable grim ending. And, indeed, huge crowds gathered to watch the poor wretches hanged. Execution days, of which there were eight per year, usually on Mondays, were often granted as official public holidays. One enterprising woman saw the opportunity to make money out of these occasions and built grandstands known as Mother Procter's Pews, which were used by the rich who had come to enjoy the spectacle in comfort. Those less-wealthy stood in their thousands to gawp at the free entertainment.

This roundel set into a road island at a busy road junction marks the place where "Tyburn Tree" – the gallows – once stood

The unfortunate prisoners were brought to Tyburn from Newgate Prison in the City on a cart that made its way through the crowds of jeering folk who travelled the same route to see the fun (ugh!) There were various stops along the way, one at St. Giles-in-the-Fields, where the condemned were given a jug of ale to help them on their way to their pitiful end and another at St. Sepulchre's church where the minister would would ask them to repent their ill-doing, ask mercy for their souls, and the church bell would ring. Often there would be another stop at the Mason's Arms for more ale. With luck, the poor wretches would be drunk and possibly insensible by the time they reached the end of their final journey.

At Tyburn the cart would line up below the gallows, the noose would be placed around the prisoner's neck, the horse's rump would be smacked and away he'd go, leaving the wretch dangling, until he died a lingering death by suffocation. Sometimes, family and friends would rush forward and hang onto the victim's legs, pulling with all their might to quicken the death and lessen the agony. There were times when it wasn't simply pity that made them do this, it was for possession of the victim's clothes and the body before surgeons wanting it for dissection in the anatomy laboratory claimed it. What an undignified end!

Because execution days occurred only eight times each year, it meant that there could be a backlog of hangings with up to double-figures waiting to meet their end. This caused great chaos in the huge crowds and often fights broke out, pockets were picked and there was a collapse of civil order, no doubt which added to the entertainment value for those sitting in the stands. It took one of the hangmen, Thomas Derrick, to come up with a solution: hang the prisoners more than one at a time. He devised a tripod, on each of the three sides of which three people could be hanged simultaneously, as three were placed in each cart. The tripod became known as a derrick and today we can still see it, often in dockland, as part of the modern cranes. Many of the onlookers claimed they were being cheated out of their gruesome enjoyment but it quickened the proceedings and those who had to "dance the Tyburn jig" did not to have to wait so long to meet their Maker.

While hanging was the main means of execution at Tyburn, there were some who were burnt there, heretics usually, and others who were hanged, drawn and quartered. Beheading was usually kept for Tower Hill and those nobles who were deemed worthy of so swift a death.

It was not until 1783 that the authorities decided to move the gallows and the executions back into the City at Newgate Jail. This was because of the riotous behaviour of the attendant mob and the need to remove the gallows, which had become an obstacle to traffic. By this time there had been some "improvements" in the method of hanging, a newly designed gallows meant that there was a longer drop so that the criminal broke his neck sooner and death was quicker than the short-drop which lead to his suffocation. Such civilised refinement!

Today all that remains of this dreaded place where the hanging of such people as Jack Sheppard the highwayman attracted a crowd of over 200,000 is a circular plaque in the traffic island where Bayswater and the Edgware roads meet.

In a Monastery Garden

With a name like Anton Vodorinsky, you'd have thought the composer (born in 1875 and died in 1959) was of Russian or Eastern European birth, but no, he was born in Birmingham and took the pseudonym Albert Ketelby by which he is better known to those of us who like his light, tuneful orchestral pieces, such as *In a Persian Market Place*, *Sanctuary of the Heart* and, a great favourite in its day, *In a Monastery Garden*. I'm sure, he would have been triply pleased to know that not one, not two, but three of the monastery gardens of Westminster Abbey are open to the public each summer on Open Squares Day, the event that is organised by the London Parks and Gardens Trust from its head-quarters at the delightfully named Duck Island Cottage in St James' Park.

When Edward the Confessor became King in 1040, because he was unable to keep a vow he had made to make a pilgrimage to Rome, he instead founded a monastery on Thorney Island, a marsh that is better known today as Westminster, where there was already a small Benedictine settlement. Since then the Collegiate Church of St. Peter (as it is correctly termed) has played a central role in British history. Many of our monarchs have been crowned there and not a few, including Elizabeth I and her cousin, Mary Queen of Scots, are buried there too,

In College Garden is this knot garden, the spaces filled with blue and white lavender. In the surrounding borders are medicinal plants, some of which are planted in pots and urns

St. Catherine's Garden was originally part of the monastery infirmary. The saint herself looks down niche on the north wall

as are famous men of science and the arts such as Sir Isaac Newton and Edmund Spenser. A national shrine where we honour those of our compatriots who died for our country and have no known grave, the Tomb of the Unknown Warrior, takes centre place in the nave. It is a special place for us.

Apart from being the burial place of the great and the good and playing its part in the ceremonial life of the nation, the Abbey has numerous treasures of which many people are unaware, not least its gardens, which come as a pleasant surprise to those who find them for the first time. Who'd have thought there was so much green and fecund space tucked away amid all the glorious architecture? Some of the gardens are open frequently but others are only open to the public on that special day in summer.

Although three gardens (Dean's Yard, St. Catherine's Garden and College Garden) are opened for the day, it is possible to see, but not to enter because it is private, the Little Cloister Garden. There, behind wrought-iron railings, is a sparkling fountain surrounded by flower beds and clipped box topiary. The residents who enjoy this tiny jewel-like oasis are lucky. It is an appetizing morsel of things to come.

Dean's Yard is a garden on the site of the former farmyard of the monastery. Surrounded by handsome buildings, the central green area is now more open than it was originally when there were more avenues of trees. Although the space has more scattered tree-cover, it is still a welcome respite from the noisome world outside… as a monastery should be.

St. Catherine's Garden was part of the infirmary and

reminders of its previous use can still be seen. The saint herself, with the wheel on which she was martyred, looks down from her niche on the north wall onto a small, enclosed, private space which has a raised border bright with the appropriate seasonal flowers. Surrounded by Abbey buildings and overlooked by the Houses of Parliament, it has all the elements and attractions of a secret garden and is entered through an arched doorway in an ancient wall.

The largest space is College Garden, which has been under continuous cultivation since before the Normans arrived in 1066. Herbs used in medicines were grown here, as was food for the monks. Grape vines and fruit trees were grown and the kitchen garden produced vegetables such as beans, leeks, and many others. The garden was large enough for the harvesting of hay. The monastery gardens are so extensive that the grounds can be seen some considerable distance away in Victoria Street, where one of the roads leading off it is called Abbey Orchard Road. At one time the Abbey owned Covent Garden, but after the Dissolution of the Monasteries by Henry VIII in 1539 the property passed to the Russell family, Earls of Bedford.

College Garden is dominated by five gigantic plane trees, Platanus x hispanicus, the oldest living things in the garden, planted in 1850. They give welcome shade on a summer's day while you sit on benches donated by the likes of the Women's Institute and others grateful for the peace of the place. Doubtless, in days gone by, the monks took exercise here amid the plants and trees, one of which, a huge fig, Ficus carica, dominates one side of the quadrangle.

The Victoria Tower of the Houses of Parliament overlooks the "monastery" garden.

A more modern development is the clipped box edges which are filled, in season, with blue and white lavender around which are borders with medicinal plants, some of which are also contained in pots and urns. The Abbey Library has record of a herbarium being constructed in 1306, perhaps on the site of the present knot garden. In the borders are such herbs as lavender, St. John's Wort, liquorice, marigold, and many others which would have been used by the monks in medicines. Today, because of the high lead content of the soil, they are grown for show rather than as cures for ailments.

College Garden, while mindful of its historic past, hasn't remained preserved in amber: a new, attractive fountain has been constructed in one corner up against the dormitory block of Westminster School, to celebrate the jubilee of the accession of Queen Elizabeth I. In another corner, a cupola garden has been developed where roses, boxhedges, beech, and hornbeam provide an attractive focal point.

The Abbey Gardens offer tranquillity for residents and visitors alike, but one is never far from the business of state for looming over the rooftops and ancient walls is the Victoria Tower of the Palace of Westminster and, a little further away, Big Ben can be seen. Nevertheless, next time you're in town, nip into the gardens for a quiet half-hour – perhaps you'll find what the monks sought, peace for meditation and rejuvenation of the spirit.

The African Roscius

In the Evangelical Cemetery in Lodz, Poland, lie the remains of a man who was awarded the Prussian Gold Medal for Arts and Sciences by King Frederick William III, the Maltese Cross from Berne in Switzerland, and the Golden Cross of Leopold from the Tsar of Russia. As if those were not recognition enough, the same man has a bronze plaque at the Shakespeare Memorial Theatre at Stratford-upon-Avon and is listed among the one hundred Greatest African Americans. And yet, until comparatively recently, he was unknown in the UK where he gave some of his greatest performances in classical roles. It was not until October 2007, two hundred years after his birth, that English Heritage unveiled, on the wall of a modest semi-detached house in Hamlet Road, Penge, south-east London, one of their blue plaques to Ira Aldridge, the African Roscius, who had once lived there.

Ira Aldridge was born on July 24th, 1807, in New York to the Reverend Daniel Aldridge and his wife, Luranah. He attended the African Free School in New York where he developed an interest in acting, which was encouraged by school visits to the Park Theatre where he watched the performances from the balcony. His first professional part was as Rolla, a Peruvian, in the play *Pizarro*, with the African Grove, an African-

American company, and it was not long before he went on to his first major Shakespearean role as Romeo and later as Hamlet. However, racist pressure forced the closure of the African Grove and, at the age of seventeen, Aldridge migrated to Britain where he hoped to have a better chance to express his dramatic talents.

Although his first job in the British theatre was as a dresser to the actor Henry Wallack, he soon began appearing in dramatic roles, performing scenes from *Othello* which pleasantly surprised many of the critics, one of whom wrote, "In 'Othello' he delivers the most difficult passages with a degree of correctness that surprises the beholder".

In 1825 he appeared in a lead role at London's Coburg Royal Theatre (now The Old Vic) as Oroonoko in *The Revolt at Surinam*. His reception was mixed but he went on to play Gambia in *The Slave's Revenge* and the title role in *Othello*. It was not only in black roles that he appeared: he took the title role in Shakespeare's *Richard III* and Shylock in *The Merchant of Venice*. He was called by some "the African Roscius" after Quintas Roscius Gallus (c. 126-62 BC) the Roman actor of such celebrity that his name became an epithet for any successful actor. Praise indeed.

And yet because of continuing adverse criticism in the Press – *The Times* even claimed that he couldn't pronounce English properly because of "the shape of his lips", Aldridge began to find it difficult to get roles so he toured the provinces where he was better received, often playing to full houses in many non-black roles such as Macbeth and King Lear. He widened his repertoire by playing in comedies, operettas, and melodramas (of which the Victorians were very fond).

The plaque outside the house where Ira Aldridge "The African Roscius" Lived on Hamlet Road, Penge, south-east London.

Notwithstanding his success elsewhere, the London stage still boycotted him so in 1857 he went to Europe to try his hand.

He was a great success. Wherever he went he was rapturously received, especially in Sweden, Russia, Poland, and the Austro-Hungarian Empire. When he finally returned to England, heaped with honours, the theatre could no longer ignore him and he appeared at the Lyceum, one of London's largest and most prestigious theatres in 1858.

Aldridge wasn't only an actor; he was a spokesman for his race. Having suffered racist criticism for most of his acting career, he would often play his guitar and sing an anti-slavery song at the end of his performances. The Abolitionist movement in England claimed this as a significant contribution to the struggle for the abolition of the slave trade.

Aldridge became a British citizen in 1863 and continued successfully touring the continent and claiming great appreciation from packed houses wherever he played. He died in Lodz, in Poland in 1867. At his funeral the whole town turned out to mourn the passing of this great actor. He was buried with State honours. His grave is a national shrine and is cared for by the Society of Polish Artists of Film and Theatre and, most appropriately, he is memorialised at Stratford, the home of Shakespeare, many of whose characters he had played to such great effect.

English Heritage erected its first Blue Plaque to Lord Byron, the poet who, like Aldridge, went without honour for many years. It now has more than eight hundred plaques around London and Ira Aldridge's is a worthy addition. How appropriate also that it should be on a house in Hamlet Road. I'm sure he would have appreciated the irony.

Coade

What's 13 feet long, 12 feet high, weighs over 13 tons, and was once bright red? I'll give you a clue: ROAR!

I bet if you were asked to name any of the statues between the National Theatre and Westminster Bridge, it wouldn't be Frank Dobson's *London Pride* which stands outside the theatre or the *Neon Tower* on the Hayward Gallery by Philip Vaughan and Roger Dainton and, almost certainly, not one of the three Dali bronzes that once stood outside what was once County Hall. I bet the one most people would remember would be the South Bank Lion at the south-eastern corner of the bridge. And rightly so.

This stretch of riverside walk was once full of thriving industries, including many breweries, one of which was the Lion Brewery or as it was sometimes known, the Red Lion Brewery because of the lion of heroic size that once stood on the entablature of the five-storey building facing the river. There was another, smaller lion on the landward side too. Both were painted red.

It was a local landmark and such was its prominence that Emile Zola, the French novelist, while staying in London in 1893 said that "It amused me greatly, this British lion waiting to wish me a good morning". And when you consider that the

The South Bank Lion – made of Coade stone

lion was placed on the brewery in May 1837 and still retains its crisp, clear details all these years later, it must have been made of some special material and been designed by some exceptional craftsmen to have withstood the ravages of time.

The South Bank, now full of entertainment venues: the Festival Hall, the British Film Institute, The Royal National Theatre, biggest crowd-puller of all, the London Eye, and many more, is built upon land which was once busy with workers rather than the tourists that flock there today. One of the main employers of these artisans who came from Lambeth, Vauxhall and other south of the river boroughs was "Mrs Coade's Artificial Stone Company".

Mrs. Eleanor Coade (1733-1821), originally from Dorset, moved to London with her family when her father went bankrupt in 1759. Ten years later she set up a factory making

A good example of the use of Coade stone is this portico on Schomberg House in Pall Mall

artificial stone at Narrow Wall, Lambeth on the bank of the Thames where the Festival Hall now stands.

Although there were other types of artificial stone (cement, stucco and the like), Coadestone, as it came to be called, had a secret formula that made it impervious to the inclemencies of the London weather such as rain, frost, and the ever-present pollution from the domestic and industrial chimneys which belched out their filth from coal fires day after day.

Mrs. Coade called her product "Lythodipyra" from the Greek for "stone twice fired". It was really a type of terracotta with a creamy surface that looks best unpainted. Its great success owed much to the building boom that was going on in London and the country at the time. Another of its properties, besides being weather resistant, is that it can, when used by

The Coade stone tomb of Captain Bligh in St. Mary's churchyard, Lambeth – now the Garden Museum

skilled craftsmen produce fine detailing for statues and facades. This made it an expensive building material, which accounts for it being used mainly by the rich and powerful. It can be found on Buckingham Palace, St. Paul's Cathedral, Castle Howard, the Old Royal Naval College at Greenwich, and many other notable buildings.

A myth has arisen that the formula for the "stone" was so secret that it died with Mrs. Coade. This is not so, for in 2000, Stephen Pettifer, a young artist who had studied sculpture and stone carving at the City and Guilds of London Art School, set up Coade Ltd. to revive the use of the medium. When I wrote to him to ask about this myth of Coadestone being lost to us today, he very kindly replied that there are a few laboratories around the world which would be able to analyse the original mix and work out its ingredients. This part is easy. It is the knowledge of what to do with the clay (Coade mix) that was lost. It is a difficult and complex process which, thankfully, he has mastered. He works to a very high standard and the National Trust, English Heritage, and Westminster Abbey have been among his many customers.

Which brings us back to the South Bank Lion. When that whole river-front area of Lambeth was being demolished to make way for the 1951 Festival of Britain, the old Lion Brewery was demolished but, by the intervention of King George VI, the lion was saved. It was first placed at ground level for passers-by to see close up, and then moved to outside Waterloo Station. It now stands on its plinth at the south-east corner of Westminster Bridge where it is much admired and used as a backdrop for the thousands of photographs that tourists take of each other I am sure that Emile Zola would still be amused to be greeted each morning by the crisp and clean South Bank Lion.

A Chaotic Quarter of Ruffianism

Some two hundred years ago, a workman, digging at a busy crossroads off the Ratcliff Highway in the East End of London, came across the remains of a corpse with a stake driven through its heart. It was not the body of a vampire, as you may surmise, but that of John Williams, suspected of the notorious Ratcliff Highway murders of December 1811

The first murders were those of Timothy Marr, a linen draper, his wife, their three-month old son and their young male shop assistant. Fortunately for her, another servant had been sent out to buy oysters. When she returned, the gruesome scene was discovered. There was public outcry. The government offered 500 guineas as a reward for the capture of the killer.

But it didn't end there, for twelve days later at The King's Arms, a pub in what was then New Gravel Lane, the publican, his wife and a female servant were slaughtered. Once again, there was an escapee – a lodger, who climbed out of a window half-naked and raised the public by crying out "They are murdering people in the house". The murders had been particularly vicious as the murderer used a chisel and maul on his victims.

After much questioning of many people, and although the evidence was circumstantial, suspicion fell on a sailor, John

Hawksmoor's church, St. George in the East where some of the victims of the Ratcliff Highway murders are burried

Williams who had once been a shipmate of the linen draper, Timothy Marr. Williams was arrested and charged but hanged himself before being brought to trial. His body was dragged behind a cart through the East End streets before a stake was driven through his heart. He was then flung into a pit where Cable Street met Cannon Street Road, crossroads being the traditional place for such unfortunates.

It was the remains of Williams' corpse that was to give the road-digger such a fright one hundred years later. After the discovery, they were shared out between those who collected such grisly remains, the skull ended up on display in a nearby pub. Some of the corpses of the unfortunate victims were buried in Hawksmoor's St. George in the East, the white stone church which has dominated the area since it was built in 1729, and still does despite being bombed in the Second World War and refashioned in the interior while keeping the splendid eighteenth century exterior.

King Edward VII Memorial Park – the memorial to those navigators who explored the northern seas in the sixteenth century

The Highway, as it now called, is in the Borough of Tower Hamlets. Originally a Roman road, this mile long major arterial highway leads from the City to Limehouse and then on to Canary Wharf and its burgeoning financial centre. It has a long and colourful history, for beside the sensational murders of 1811, it had a notorious reputation for crime and vice. The author Thomas De Quincey (1785-1859), better known for his *Confessions of an English Opium Eater*, wrote in his satirical essay "The Fine Art of Murder" that Ratcliff was "a most chaotic quarter... and an area of manifold ruffianism."

Its name, "Ratcliff" is derived from the Saxon for "red cliff" and it was known as a centre of shipbuilding and those trades which serviced it. John Stow, the sixteenth century English chronicler, mentions it in his *Survey of London and Westminster* (1598) as being "a filthy strait passage with alleys of small tenements". In later centuries, beside the increase of the population, nothing much had changed and in Victorian

St. Katherine's Dock – "The Grand Turk" a replica 18th Century frigate near "The Highway"

times Oscar Wilde travelled along the Ratcliff Highway to visit opium dens, as did Arthur Conan Doyle when doing research for his most famous creation, Sherlock Holmes, who was fond of a pipe of opium (as well as an injection of a 7% solution of cocaine) which could be found in this overcrowded area full of brothels, bars, and drug dens, all vying to part sailors and others from their wallets.

But there is more to the history of this part of Wapping than casual slaughter. At 179-180, opposite Artichoke Hill, was Jamrach's – a kind of animal supermarket where you could hire or buy exotic creatures: perhaps pop in for a penguin, pick up a lion with the daily newspaper or browse the aisles for a python or okapi (I wonder if they did special offers,

"Two emus for the price of one". Stacking the shelves must have presented some problems). At one time a tiger escaped and was seen strolling along the Highway with a local youth in his mouth. The poor boy was killed not by the tiger but by the man who attempted to rescue him, for in trying to prise the tiger's lunch from its jaws, the boy was bashed on the bonce and expired. Well, that's one version of the story. Another version has Mr. Jamrach forcing apart the tiger's jaws and freeing the unfortunate youth who, it is claimed, was eventually given £300 compensation, a fortune in those days, while the tiger was lead back to the emporium.

Until the closure of the docks in the 1960's, Ratcliff was a flourishing maritime community, especially at the height of the British Empire when London was the centre of ship-born world trade. There was an apocryphal claim that you could cross the Thames by walking over the decks of ships waiting to be unloaded in the Pool of London.

And before that, from Ratcliff Cross many voyages of discovery were begun. Captain James Cook lived in the area and had his children baptised at St. Paul's church, Shadwell. At 326, The Highway it is recorded that "The ablest and most renowned Navigator this or any country hath produced" lived nearby. He added greatly to the knowledge of the Pacific and the Southern Ocean as well as claiming lands such as Australia for the British Crown.

To the south of The Highway, almost opposite St. George's church, is the King Edward VII Memorial Park where a fish market once stood. At the riverside is the round ventilator shaft of the Rotherhithe Tunnel, which has on its wall a plaque, made of tiles on which it is recorded that the explorers Sir Hugh Willoughby, Stephen Borough, William Borough and Sir Martin Frobisher "set sail from this reach of the river to explore the northern seas". Willoughby and the Boroughs set out to discover a north passage to the east but Willoughby died and the Boroughs went on to explore Russia and help set up the Muscovy Company. Frobisher set out three times to discover a north-west passage to Cathay but he failed to do so. He was more successful in his services against the Armada, for which he was knighted.

The Rotherhithe Tunnel ventilator shaft is a memorial not only to these hardy navigators but also to an endeavour that failed in its initial aim. The royalist exile from revolutionary France, Marc Isambard Brunel (father of you know who), when whiling away time in jail for debt had a "Robert the Bruce and the Spider" moment for he watched a shipworm chewing its way through wood and excreting the waste as it moved on. *Bingo!* thought Marc Isambard and when he was released he developed the idea of a gigantic corkscrew which like the shipworm would pass the waste material behind it as the workers shored up the lengthening tunnel which took 18 years to complete and at the price of ten men's lives. However, the foot-tunnel was not a financial success and instead of the public flocking to cross the river by this novel way, it became the haunt of whores and robbers. Eventually, it was taken over by the East London Railway in 1869 and is now part of the London Underground system.

The hamlet of Ratcliff, lying on the north bank of the Thames between Shadwell and Limehouse is no more and there is precious little left of its long and colourful history. The docks have gone, their warehouses converted into expensive apartments for those who can afford them and there is a strange emptiness and quiet in the riverside streets and alleys but if, of an evening, you stand by Wapping Old Stairs and hear the Thames lapping at your feet, it is easy to imagine Captain Blood being captured there while trying to escape with the Crown Jewels or you might even hear the crying of those who had been condemned to deportation to Australia for it was from a riverside pub, The Town of Ramsgate, that the prisoners were held in the cellars. "Sailor Town" with its bars, brothels and opium dens has gone, along with the Ratcliff Highway, which is now a dual carriageway to be avoided at busy times of day.

Dickens and the Borough

A school, square, and estate named after Dickens' characters; Copperfield, Quilp, Pickwick, Weller Streets, and Little Dorrit Court, all indicate the part played by the Borough in the life and works of the great Victorian writer. There are other places in London associated with Charles Dickens – the Old Curiosity Shop, his home in Doughty Street, Fleet Street where he worked as a journalist – but none has a greater concentration of connections than Southwark and the Borough on the south bank of the Thames. Shakespeare's Globe Theatre was here and it was the starting point for Geoffrey Chaucer's pilgrims as they wended their way to Canterbury "the holy blissful martyr for to seeke", but it is Dickens who can claim to have inhabited the area with many characters in his books and for it to play a significant part in his own life.

Borough High Street, known as "The Borough", has been a busy thoroughfare since Roman times. It led to the only bridge over the Thames until 1750 and all traffic met there. The road was full of coaching inns, all catering for the needs of those travelling to and from the capital. It also met other needs and was where you came for theatres, the cock and bear pits and, of course, the stews or brothels. It was a combustible mix and John Wesley called part of it "a nursery of all manner of wickedness".

The Church of St. George the Martyr (left). In "Little Dorrit" Dickens has the heroine spend a night sleeping in the vestry with a register as her pillow when she returns too late and the doors of the Marshalsea are locked and The George Inn, Southwark, London (right) which is also mentioned by Dickens in "Little Dorrit"

To counteract such wickedness, the Borough was also the site of several prisons: the King's Bench Prison where Titus Oates, fabricator of the Popish Plot of 1685, was jailed, as was the radical politician John Wilkes; poor old Mr. Micawber was visited by David Copperfield while languishing there when "his difficulties came to a crisis"; there was the House of Correction in St. George's Fields; the Horsemonger Lane Jail saw the poet and publisher Leigh Hunt within its walls for calling the Prince Regent "a fat Adonis of fifty" and, more importantly, it was there that Dickens witnessed the hanging of Mr. and Mrs. Manning for the murder of a friend for his money: Dickens was so appalled by the behaviour of the crowd that he wrote in a letter to *The Times* – "The horrors of the gibbet and of the crime which brought the wretched murderers to it, faded in my mind before the atrocious bearing, looks and language of the number of spectators." Thus began the campaign for the ending of public executions. They ended in 1868 when J. T. Hibbert MP successfully introduced a Private Member's Bill to abolish them.

But it was the Marshalsea Prison that Dickens had most acquaintance with. It derived its name from the court held by the Marshall of the King's Household and was founded in 1371. It saw some distinguished inmates. Walter Raleigh had been jailed there for a punch-up at the tennis court in Westminster. The playwright Thomas Nashe was slung in there along with his actors for a seditious play, *The Isle of Dogs*. And the Headmaster of Eton, Nicholas Udall (1504-1556), author of what is recognised as the first English comedy *Ralph Roister Doister*, was banged-up for buggery and theft of the college silver. Strangely, he confessed to the first charge because it was not regarded as serious as the second and had a lesser sentence. It did not seem to affect his career for King Edward VI made him a prebendary of Windsor.

However, in 1824, Charles' father, John Dickens, was jailed in the Marshalsea for debt. He had been a clerk in the Navy Office in Portsmouth where Charles was born but moved to London with his job and then again to Chatham where he was made redundant. This was the beginning of his money troubles. The family moved to a small house in Camden Town but even that did not help solve their problems, which stemmed from John being financially irresponsible. His wife was forever pawning goods to avoid disaster. To little avail, for her husband was imprisoned twice for debt. The whole family went with him with the exception of Charles who was set to work in Warren's Blacking Factory at 30, Strand (where Charing Cross Station now stands), sticking labels on pots of blacking (polish) for shoes. It was a dismal place where rats could be heard scrabbling beneath the floorboards. Each day, the twelve-year-old Charles would leave his lodgings in Lant Street and breakfast with his family in the Marshalsea before trudging across London Bridge to the hated place of work.

The old medieval bridge, over 600 years old, was demolished in 1831 and a new one by John Rennie, replaced it. Gone were the alcoves that lined the old bridge (though one can still be seen in the grounds of Guy's Hospital nearby in which sits a bronze figure of the poet Keats who was a student at the hospital). The young Charles would sometimes sit in one of these alcoves and witness teeming humanity as it passed by on its business. His acute observation and retentive memory furnished him with a wealth of material for his stories and novels. In *David Copperfield*, the eponymous hero at one time sits in such a recess and in *Great Expectations*, Pip crosses the bridge shocked by the news that Estela and Drummle are betrothed. At the south-west corner of the bridge one flight of steps which leads down to Montague Close is known as "Nancy's Steps" for it was here that in *Oliver Twist* Nancy secretly (or so she thought) met Mr. Brownlow before she is betrayed by the Artful Dodger and brutally murdered by Bill Sikes (who later meets his own death in Jacob's Island – the filthy riverside rookery, which is, in reality, Jacob's Street).

The remaining wall of Marshalsea Prison

Victorian Southwark's population rapidly increased and there was gross overcrowding in squalid tenements and dingy backstreets. It was observed by W. Booth that here, as in other developing quarters of the capital, "Famine, Filth and Disease were rife in the richest city on God's earth". Plenty of folk, not only of the Borough, but all of London, ended up in one of the many jails. Like Dickens' father, Amy Dorrit's also found himself in the Marshalsea along with his family. They could go in and out freely and one evening poor Little Dorrit was too late back at the prison and the gates were closed against her. She slept in the vestry of the nearby church of St. George the Martyr where she used one of the registers as her pillow. Later in the story she marries Arthur Clenham there. In the east window of the church is a small stained-glass window of her.

Ironically, John Dickens' family found it cheaper to live in prison because he had no rent to pay. Charles, however, was mortified by his father's imprisonment and was embarrassed by it all his life. So much so that once when a friend, Bob

Fagin, accompanied him from work because he was unwell and left him at the corner of his street, Charles knocked at another, stranger's door in case his workmate was watching. The spectre of debt and poverty lingered at Dickens' shoulder all his life, even when he had become the most famous and successful writer in the world.

But it is not only the remains of the Marshalsea, off Angel Court, that remind us of Dickens and his works. The George, the only galleried inn left in London and owned by the National Trust, is mentioned in *Little Dorrit* and in one of its bars in a glassed fame is the author's life insurance policy.

Near the north end of the Borough, hard against the Thames, is Southwark Cathedral, the parish church of St. Saviour in the nineteenth century, which is mentioned in another of his stories, *The Uncommercial Traveller*.

In a long and not always happy journey from the blacking factory to national mourning and burial in Westminster Abbey, Dickens gave us a spectrum of unforgettable characters drawn from many places, not least of which is Southwark and the Borough.

England's Michelanglo and the Unsung Heroes

In 1884 the English artist George Frederic Watts (1817-1904 and so called because he was born on Handel's birthday), was the first living artist to be given a solo exhibition at the Metropolitan Museum of Art, New York. It was such a success that its run was extended by six months and led to Watts giving to the American people his painting *Love and Life* which President Theodore Roosevelt had placed in the White House.

Watts' influence continued, albeit indirectly and non-artistically, over a century later with the favourite painting of Barack Obama, *Hope* by the same artist which was brought to his attention by his then pastor, the Rev Wright, in a sermon in which he referred to the melancholy picture of a blindfolded girl sitting atop the world and plucking at a simple one-string lyre. Wright used the phrase "the woman had the audacity to hope". You can see why such an emotive phrase appealed to the man who went on to become the first black American President who entitled his second book *The Audacity of Hope*.

Obama was not the only black man to find resonance in Watts' painting. Nelson Mandela kept a reproduction of it on his cell wall while imprisoned on Robben Island.

Memorial plaques in Postman's Park

And what of Watts today? Who remembers the artist who was awarded the Order of Merit by Queen Victoria and was a member of the Royal Academy? He was even compared to the greatest of the Renaissance masters and, in his time, was called "England's Michelangelo"?

His beginnings were modest. He was born in the London district of Marylebone, the son of a poor piano-maker who taught him a literal interpretation of Christianity, which Watts later rejected, and classics such as *The Iliad*, which were later to influence his work. He showed artistic promise from his early years and claimed that it was because of his study of the Elgin Marbles that he "alone learned".

He became a gifted sculptor, landscape artist, portraitist and symbolist whose influence can be seen in the works of artists such as: Ferdinand Knopf, the Belgian symbolist; Gustave Moreau; Rodin, the great French sculptor; and, it is claimed, even that giant of twentieth century art, Pablo Picasso.

Watts belonged to no school; he was his own man. Philosopher as well as artist, he believed that art had an important part to play in educating mankind, in opening the eyes of his fellow beings to the eternal truths of Life, and as a means of social reform in an age that was losing its faith and in which such problems as poverty, child prostitution and cruelty to animals were rife. Many of his works have a social and moral dimension, such as the paintings he did of the Irish Famine and those showing Victorian poverty e. g. *The Song of the Shirt* and *Found Drowned*. Others have an allegorical content, such as *Industry and Greed*, *Mammon*, and, of course, perhaps his most famous of all, *Hope*, reproductions of which were found in many homes.

While in his own time he was considered the greatest painter of the Victorian era, his reputation has since fallen and his work has been thought mawkish and too sentimental for today's taste, but interest in him was resurrected by the BBC programme *Restoration* and, as a result, his gallery at Compton, near Guildford, received grants for refurbishment – this unique English gem is well worth a visit.

However, if you can't get there to appreciate the uniqueness of Watts, then in the City of London, tucked behind the church of St. Botolph-without-Aldersgate and the post office in King Edward Street is Postman's Park, a welcome oasis from the bustle of City life. What makes it doubly welcome are the ceramic plaques placed under cover on a wall that commemorate those ordinary folk, many of them children, who gave their lives to save others. There's Mary Rogers, stewardess on the *Stella Mar* who gave up her lifebelt so that someone else might be saved; George Lee, a fireman, who carried a girl to safety before succumbing to the flames himself; and Elizabeth Boxall, 17, who died trying to save a child from a runaway horse, to name but a few. All unsung heroes.

It may well be that Watts is no longer held in high esteem as an artist but it is obvious that he was a decent, high-minded man, as a visit to Postman's Park will show, for these plaques were his idea: a tribute to those who gave their lives for others and who otherwise may have done so unnoticed and unrecorded.

The Lord Mayor's Daughter and the Crossing Sweeper

Some of us of a certain age may remember an old black-and-white film made in 1950 by 20th Century Fox called *The Mudlark*. It starred Irene Dunne as Queen Victoria, Alec Guinness as her Prime Minister, Disraeli, and Andrew Ray as the eponymous mudlark, a young boy who, with others, made his living by scavenging on the Thames foreshore in between tides, very often for washed up pieces of coal which they collected in baskets and sold in the streets for pennies. The eventual encounter and relationship between the Widow of Windsor and one of her poorest subjects caused the beginning of her emergence from her extended mourning for her beloved Consort, Prince Albert.

Victorian London was not a pleasant place for the poor and many made their livings from the most meagre of sources. There were bone-pickers, rag-collectors, "pure finders" who collected dog excrement for the tanning trade, "toshers" who hunted the sewers for things of value, and those who did the same in great mounds of litter and dust, but most numerous and visible of all were the crossing-sweepers. So well-known were they that they appeared in paintings and books: William Powell-Frith's *The Crossing-Sweeper* was a print found in

The obelisk erected in memory of Robert Walthman, M.P. and Lord Mayor of London

many homes and Dickens' Jo in *Bleak House*, one of his most popular characters, was a crossing-sweeper.

When you remember that the "horseless carriage" had yet to give us the full-scale of its mixed blessings and that the Victorian capital of empire was a horse town with over 300,000 of the animals in the streets, 10,000 of which were plying for public business, it is easy to see why crossing-sweepers were needed. Ladies in their fine, long dresses and cloaks and with expensive, delicate footwear and gentlemen, especially in the city, in equally expensive and highly-polished boots and shoes and sharply-creased trousers, were in need of the services provided by the crossing-sweepers.

That they performed a useful service was not agreed by all. In his voluminous study *London Labour and the London*

Poor the journalist Henry Mayhew saw crossing-sweeping as a "resort for begging". In some well-used areas there were so many sweepers that it was cheaper to take the omnibus to one's destination rather than pay every sweeper you met. The Strand and Fleet Street was such an example. It was estimated that there were about 35 sweepers along this length of highway.

Not everyone complained. There were those who supported the "work" done by these urchins and indigent poor. Shopkeepers liked to have the pavement and roadway in front of their premises kept clean, for it helped their businesses and many paid crossing-sweepers a small retainer to ensure this.

In New York where there were sweepers too, one irate matron wrote to *The New York Times* complaining when the city passed a law prohibiting them for, she said, they helped clear the snow when there had been a heavy fall and sometimes in the winter it was impossible to cross to the other side of the street "without sinking to the ankle".

Many London crossing-sweepers had permanent pitches, the same stretch of road and pavement that they regularly attended. They became known to local pedestrians and shopkeepers alike.

One such was Charles McGhee, a native of Jamaica whose pitch was at the busy junction of Ludgate Hill and Fleet Street. He was a distinctive character with one eye, grey hair tied back in a bunch and, unlike many sweepers, comparatively well-dressed for he wore an old frock-coat, presumably given to him by a grateful pedestrian.

He was doubly fortunate in his choice of pitch, for not only was it busy, but it was also outside a popular and successful linen-draper's shop. Its owner, Robert Waithman, a Welshman who entered both local and national politics, became MP for the City of London, Sheriff of Middlesex, and eventually Lord Mayor. He was in favour of political reform and could often be heard in the coffee houses of the City airing his views, including opposition to the French War, which did not endear him to many who had vested interest in keeping the status quo. He was called "the friend of liberty in evil times and of parliamentary reform in its adverse days".

From her place in an upstairs window, Waithman's daughter would watch Charles McGee going about his work each day. No matter what the weather was like he was always there, polite and serviceable. Often she would send out food for him, especially during the winter when he was given bowls of hot soup and chunks of bread.

One day when she noticed his absence, she made enquiries and found out that he had died. She was saddened by this news but this was followed by surprise when she learned that he had left all his savings to her, over £700, a great sum in those Victorian days, especially one made from sweeping crossings. Her kindness had not been forgotten.

Waithman's shop is long gone and the obelisk that was erected to honour him by his "friends and fellow citizens" and which once stood near it on Ludgate Circus has been moved to Salisbury Court, off Fleet Street, near Saint Bride's Church where he is buried. His good works are thus remembered but it would be a shame if those of his daughter to the crossing-sweeper were to be forgotten.

Somewhat of a Cockney

On a summer's day, June 23rd, 1869, behind the Royal Exchange in the heart of Britain's financial centre, the City of London, in what is now a pedestrianised cut-through but which was once the site of St. Benet Fink (one of Wren's post-Great Fire churches that was demolished in 1842), Queen Victoria's eldest son, heir to the throne and bane of her life, Edward, the profligate and promiscuous Prince of Wales, unveiled a statue of George Peabody, merchant, financier and, most importantly for Londoners, philanthropist. He was the first American to be given the Freedom of the City of London.

Near the west door of Edward the Confessor's Collegiate Church of St. Peter, better known to most as Westminster Abbey, there is a small stone in the centre aisle on which is the following inscription:

> Here were deposited from Nov. 12th to Dec. 11th 1869, the remains of George Peabody, then removed to his native country and buried in Danvers, now Peabody, Massachusetts. "I have prayed to my Heavenly Father day by day that I might be enabled before I die to show my gratitude for the blessings which he has bestowed on me by doing some good to my fellow men.

American Philanthropist George Peabody - behind the Royal Exchange

Let your light so shine before men that they may see your good works and glorify your Father which is in Heaven."

What had this man of humble birth and Unitarian stock done to deserve a statue in the City and temporary burial amid the tombs of royalty and the great and the good of British history?

George Peabody was born in 1795, the son of poor parents who apprenticed him to a local grocer. He took to the trade and was so successful that he went on to set up his own dry goods business in Baltimore in 1814. It flourished and many more branches were opened across the United States of America.

In 1827 he visited England, not only to find markets for his own goods but to buy produce as well, such as cotton from the Lancashire mills. This venture, too, was successful, so much so that he opened a branch of Peabody in Liverpool. The British business grew to such an extent that, in 1837, George Peabody settled in London for the last thirty years of his life. He branched out into the finance and banking business and became a partner of Junius Spencer Morgan, and their firm became the ancestor of such firms as J. P. Morgan Chase, Morgan Grenfell and Morgan Stanley, all formed sometime after Peabody retired from the firm in 1864, a very wealthy man.

Peabody liked his adopted country, especially London, and called himself "somewhat of a Cockney". Although his great wealth enabled him to mix with such people as the Rothschilds and Lord Shaftesbury, he lived quite simply in rented rooms and enjoyed singing Scottish ballads and going out into society to play backgammon.

As pleasant as these aspects of his life were, Peabody was disturbed by the plight of the London poor. The change from an agrarian economy to an industrial one meant that the capital was expanding as people flocked to it in the hope of making a living. Consequently, there was gross over-crowding and conditions in such districts as Whitechapel, Spitalfields and Bethnal Green were so bad that they became congested breeding grounds for typhoid, cholera, and crime. The better-off people in the West End knew little or nothing of this and, as one contemporary clergyman said, "The East End is as little known as Kamchatka."

Peabody wanted to do something useful with his money. He first thought of installing fountains, a ready source of clean water, then he pondered schools for the hoards of children who lived in squalor and often worked long hours for little pay to help eke out their families' lives of hopeless drudgery. However, Lord Shaftesbury, another Christian philanthropist, suggested that he devote funds to the housing of the city's poor. And thus Peabody's involvement with bettering the lot of the London poor was born.

In 1862 the Peabody Donation Fund was established with a capital of £150,000 and the objective of helping to house, not the unemployed and destitute as is often thought, but those of good character and in steady employment, however humble. The first dwellings, five-storey blocks of flats, were opened in 1863 in Commercial Street, Spitalfields. There were areas for the children to play safely, laundry facilities, and shared toilets. Accommodation cost 2/6 for a single room, 4/- for two rooms and 5/- for three rooms. Unsurprisingly, there was no shortage of applicants.

Every member of each family had to be vaccinated; the common parts (stairs, landings, lavatories and windows) had to be washed every Saturday morning, and anyone not abiding by the rules had to leave. Very few risked eviction because, compared to what they had known, these flats were pure luxury. The philanthropic American gave an added £500,000 to the Fund, and between 1870 and 1885 fifteen more blocks of Peabody Buildings were opened and became a common sight across London.

In his own country he did a lot of good also, benefitting educational bodies, especially those for freed slaves in the Southern States of the USA. Peabody's philanthropy was celebrated in Britain when he was given the Freedom of the City of London in recognition of his contribution to the London poor. He was offered a baronetcy but graciously refused, saying that all he wanted was a letter of commendation from the Queen's own hand. Victoria obliged.

Gorge Peabody died on November 4th, 1869, and although he had requested burial in his home town of Danvers, he was honoured by being given temporary burial in Westminster Abbey, at the Dean's suggestion. Prime Minister Gladstone asked Queen Victoria if his remains could be returned to America in some fitting way and she allowed her newest and largest ship, *H.M.S. Monarch*, to carry Peabody home to America – a suitable tribute to the man who had done so much for the London poor.

The housing charity that he established is now called Peabody and it continues its good work and currently provides more than 19,000 homes across London (to which its activity is confined). George Peabody's legacy lives on and the light of this "somewhat Cockney" still shines before men.

One Street

Many people have found, like Dick Whittington on his fortune-seeking first visit, that London's streets are not paved with gold. They are however full of history.

There are those who think that the name Park Street, in Southwark SE1, is a misnomer for there is precious little of a park to be found in its meandering half-mile stretch between the trendy Borough Market at its eastern end and its junction with Sumner Street at its western end. They do not realise that it got its name from the Bishop of Winchester's 70 acre parkland, which once covered the area where he had his abode. All that remains of this powerful prelate's palace is the splendid tracery of the fourteenth century rose window, part of the Great Hall which can be seen in Clink Street which is named after the notorious episcopal jail.

If we start at the Market end of Park Street and keep to the right-hand pavement, it's not long before we begin to see signs of its long and eventful history – just past the pub on the corner and high up on the wall of the three-storey house opposite, number 7, there is a plaque. The writing may be too high to see but it records that this was part of the estate of Thomas Cure, saddler to three Tudor monarchs: Edward VI, the boy king who died young: his half-sister, the Catholic Mary

I; and his other half sister, Elizabeth I. What eventful times Thomas Cure lived through. He was lucky enough not to fall foul of any one of the monarchs he was saddler to.

Perhaps it was in gratitude for such luck that Cure founded a college (hospital and almshouses) for poor people in what is now Park Street, which he endowed with his property. Like so much else in the area that had to accommodate the coming of the railway, the college and associated almshouses had to move after 300 years to new buildings in West Norwood in 1863, when the estate was bought by the Charing Cross Railway Company.

Because he had bequeathed his properties to the Parish of Saint Saviour, he was buried in the parish church, now Southwark Cathedral, where his tomb is topped by a stone cadaver, a stark reminder that as Shakespeare, (another Southwark resident at one time) said, "Golden lads and girls all must/Like chimney sweepers come to dust". On 24th May, 2011, 423 years after his death, Cure was remembered at a Sung Evensong in the Cathedral and a wreath was laid on his tomb.

Slightly further on, the street takes a northward turn towards the river before bending yet again towards Southwark Bridge. It was along this stretch that the chief industry of the area, brewing, was concentrated. A plaque on pillar tells us that for over 300 years there were five owners of the Anchor Brewery, starting with James Monger in 1616 and ending with Courage in 1981. The Thrale family who owned it at one time were great friends with Dr. Samuel Johnson, the famous lexicographer.
It was during the ownership of Barclay Perkins & Co. that the brewery became the largest in the world. In 1815 they

produced 333,000 barrels of ale. However, in May 1832 a disastrous fire destroyed much of the brewery. This was not without its blessings, for it enabled the owners to rebuild and extend the brewery and turn it into one of the visitor attractions of its day. Such was its fame that the Prince of Wales came to visit and, perhaps, partake of the chief product, its well-known Russian Stout. Other famous visitors were Prince Louis-Napoléon Bonaparte, Ibrahim Pasha of Egypt, Giuseppe Garibaldi, the Italian Nationalist, and Otto von Bismarck, the Chancellor of Germany, about whose visit the following, probably apocryphal, tale is told. In 1885 the Iron Chancellor, on a diplomatic visit to London, was taken to see the sights, including Barclay's brewery. He was offered a tankard of the strongest brew and downed the lot. Another full tankard was offered which Bismarck also poured down his princely throat with relish. After the visit, as he was leaving, it is claimed that the staff cheered and applauded him, for no man before had downed two half-gallon tankards and managed not only to stay on his feet but to get to his carriage without falling over. However, on his way back to duties, having crossed the Thames, the Iron Chancellor proved only too human and, feeling the effects of the booze, told his carriage driver to stop. Whereupon Bismarck alighted and took an hour's nap on one of the Embankment benches. Can you just imagine it – the diplomatic corps in attendance waiting patiently while one of the architects of German unity snoozed beside the Thames?

Politics was to play another part in the visit of a more controversial visitor. In 1850 the Austrian General Haynau, who was notorious throughout Europe for the severity of his reprisals against those in Hungary and Italy who had rebelled against the rule of the Austro-Hungarian Empire, came to sample the brewery's ale. It had been reported that Haynau had set his men on women and children as well as opposing soldiers with such especial cruelty that he had become known as "The Hyena". When the brewery staff saw his name in the visitors' book, they attacked Haynau and his entourage who fled along Bankside and, it is claimed, took refuge in The George pub where he was rescued by the police.

There were Royal repercussions. The Austrian Ambassador demanded an apology but Lord Palmerston, the Foreign Secretary, refused to give one. In stepped an angry Queen Victoria who commanded Palmerston to apologise. He bravely refused and offered to resign. Eventually, a more conciliatory letter was sent to Vienna. One hopes that the Double-Headed Eagle was appeased. A plaque records this International Incident on a pillar where the draymen and brewery workers threw stones and attacked "The Hyena".

Further along Park Street, on land that was subsequently taken over by the brewery, is the site of one of the glories of the Elizabethan Age, the Globe Theatre. It did not stand where the present Globe now attracts many visitors and there are those who do not venture in to this back street beneath Southwark Bridge. Were they to do so, they would find a bronze image of Shakespeare and Bankside as it was in his day. We can see the Bishop's palace, the Bear Pit, the Swan and Hope Theatres and, especially prominent (as it deserves to be), the Globe – Shakespeare's own theatre.

Plaque on Park St, Southwark which records the visit of "The Austrian Butcher", Julius Von Haynau to Barclay and Perkis Brewery. He was attacked by the draymen because of his brutality towards women in the wars of Austria against Hungary and Italy. He was known as the Hyena of Brescia – a place where he had women whipped.

The Globe was home to the Lord Chamberlain's men, a group of actors later known as the King's Men, to which the Bard belonged and for whom he wrote many of his plays. In 1576, after some years in Shoreditch, this company of actors, after a disagreement with their landlord, had dismantled The Theatre as it was then known and brought it south of the river where it reopened with the name all the world knows. It was here that *Henry V*, *Anthony and Cleopatra*, *Julius Caesar*, *Hamlet*, and *Macbeth* were first performed. Glory days indeed. The polygonal building has all but disappeared beneath subsequent development but its shape is marked out in an open space between buildings and its history is told to us on accessible display panels.

Not only at the Globe but a short distance along the street, on the other side of Southwark Bridge, are the remains of the Rose Theatre, the first on Bankside, which was discovered when the site was being redeveloped for an office block. Here were first performances of Marlowe's *Doctor Faustus*, *The Jew of Malta*, *Tamburlaine the Great*, and both Shakespeare's *Henry VI: Part I* and *Titus Andronicus*. It is thought that it was the success of the Rose that encouraged other theatres to be built in this area, away from the strictures of the City of London's laws and regulations.

Not far after these discoveries, Park Street, passing the southern ends of Rose Alley and Bear Gardens, reaches its end at Sumner Street. Its short length is full of historical riches and well-worth a stroll down before you pop into one of the nearby pubs for a bevvie.

Keeping Faith

In 1666 the Great Fire razed the Square Mile of the City of London to the ground: 89 churches, 13,000 houses and 400 streets were lost. The young Christopher Wren was summoned from Oxford where he was Professor of Astronomy, and commissioned to rebuild St. Paul's Cathedral and 51 churches, though he was actually responsible for only 50. Unfortunately, during the Second World War Hitler's Luftwaffe and the Blitz reduced this number to 23.

If you stand on the traffic island at the western end of Cheapside, (once the main thoroughfare and marketplace of the capital), at its junction with Newgate Street and St. Martin-le-Grand, you will be able to see some of the remaining Wren churches and two partial ones: St. Vedast, Foster Lane; St Mary-le-Bow; St. Sepulchre-without-Newgate; Christchurch, Greyfriars; St. Paul's; and in its shadow, attached to a modern building, is another tower and spire. This is what is left of the church of St. Augustine-with-St. Faith, which was to gain a new feline parishioner in the summer of 1936.

A stray cat had been lurking around the churchyard for some time and, as cats do, she'd been trying to get into the church. Thomas Evans the verger wasn't having that and had the cat evicted a number of times. However, moggies are

St. Paul's Cathedral and St. Augustine's which is now the cathedral choir school

determined creatures and she managed to sneak in without Thomas noticing. She made her way to the rectory where she found a more sympathetic ear, that of Father Henry Ross, the Rector. He decided she should stay. He named her Faith not only after one of the church's patronal saints but because, besides tenacity, the cat had the faith to keep trying to get in.

Faith took to her new role as the church cat with great ease. No longer skinny, she became a plump presence at church services where she would sit in the pulpit at Father Ross's feet or in the front pew, looking up at her rescuer. She was a great success with the other parishioners who made a fuss of her, especially the ladies from the altar-guild who fed her titbits and helped to look after her.

Faith had her routine mapped out. Part of it was to arrive on the Rector's bed early in the morning to ask for breakfast. One morning, however, she did not put in her usual call. Intrigued and not a little worried (for this was 1940 when London was under attack from the Luftwaffe), Father Ross went to investigate. He found that he now had two cats to be responsible for. There in Faith's basket was a kitten whose arrival in church was greeted by the choir singing *All Things Bright and Beautiful*. The new arrival, a male, was called Panda because he was black and white.

Faith was a good mother, so much so that when one night she was to be seen carrying her offspring down to the basement, the Rector was puzzled and followed her down. He found that she had made a little den for herself and Panda among the hymn books and other paraphernalia stored there. He picked them up and returned them to their more usual and comfortable surroundings upstairs. This was not to be for Faith, persistent as ever, continued to take her son downstairs only for Father Ross to return them upstairs. Eventually, the cat won the battle and it was decided that if she wanted to go the basement, she could.

That evening, Henry Ross, out on his parochial duties, was unable to return home because he had to take shelter during an enemy air raid. That night, September 9th, eight churches were destroyed in the City and as he went home the Rector could not but wonder if St. Augustine's had been one of them. It had. Except for the tower and steeple, there was nothing left standing: all was a smouldering wreck.

Ignoring the firemen's warning that the area was dangerous, Father Ross clambered over the rubble looking for his beloved pets. He called out, somewhat prophetically, "Faith, Faith" until he heard an answering "Miaow". He dug away the timbers and masonry until there beneath all the destruction he found Panda and Faith, a little shaken but safe. He had just managed to get them out when a final section of roof fell where they had been. It really had been a case of Faith all round. But this was not to be the end of the of the indomitable cat's adventures.

With the passing years Panda grew up and became as much loved a pet at an old folks' home as Faith was at the church (where services were held in the tower). Her wartime rescue had been commemorated by the Rector with a photograph and tribute, which he had framed and hung in the vestry. This was brought to the attention of Maria Dickin, founder of the People's Dispensary for Sick Animals and the begetter of the Dickin Medal for Animal Bravery. However, because Faith was not a military cat she was not eligible for the medal but Maria Dickin, a deeply devoted friend of animals, thought that Faith deserved some recognition and a special silver medal was made for her. As if this was not enough, the Archbishop of Canterbury was invited to the ceremony and on October 12th, 1945, the Primate of All England, Geoffrey Fisher, held Faith while Maria Dickin placed the medal around the brave cat's neck. The citation was: "From the P. D. S. A. to Faith of St. Augustine's, Watling Street. For steadfast courage in the Battle of London, September 9th, 1940".

On September 28th, 1948, aged 14, Faith died while lying on the rug in front of the fire. The distraught Rector decided that the church cat should have a church service. He found a suitable box and lay Faith in it. The following day, in a packed church a service was duly held after which, led by the choir, the procession went into the churchyard and Faith was laid to rest at the church gate.

Eventually, St Augustine's was closed and became part of St. Paul's Choir School. The Parks Department of the City is now responsible for the upkeep of the grounds and try as I might, I have been unable to find the resting place of Faith the Church Cat. A pity, that.

Where Wolves Preyed on the Thames Bank

When the Victorian engineer and pioneer of public health, Joseph Bazalgette (1819-1891), came up with the idea of an embankment behind which sewage could be trapped and carried downstream, he not only solved the problem caused by the effluent being emptied into the Thames, but between 1864-1870 he reclaimed 37 acres of land on which the Victoria Embankment Gardens were laid out and London gained a new east-west road, making the journey from the City to Westminster much quicker and easier.

In 1890 the wealthy American, William Waldorf Astor, moved to England permanently and, in 1895, he had Astor House built at 2 Temple Place. The first Viscount Astor erected, to elaborate specifications, what has been called "an imposing casket of Portland stone" where the large warehouse of Gwynne, the pumping engineer had previously stood. Because the soil was river mud, excavations were dug forty feet into the riverbank. During these excavations the remains of oxen were found – they had been killed by wolves when they came down to the river to drink. It's difficult to imagine such scenes when strolling through the Embankment Gardens on a summer's day.

Lord Astor chose as his architect, John Loughborough Pearson, who built the glorious "cathedral of the suburbs", St.

John the Evangelist, Upper Norwood as a dry run for the first Anglican cathedral built in England since the Reformation at Truro in Cornwall.

No expense was spared: outstanding craftsmen were engaged to work the most costly materials from the carved stonework, which gave the house a Tudor appearance, to the ornamental metalwork and elaborate woodcarving of the interior. A touch of whimsy are the two cherubs which flank the entrance steps – one has an electric light bulb in his hand and the other on the phone: these modern marvels were available only to the very rich in those days.

The interior is even more impressive, for from the very entrance hall, floored with marble, porphyry and onyx, rises a magnificent solid mahogany staircase. Lord Astor was a lover of literature and on each of the newel posts on the staircase he had carved characters from his favourite novel, *The Three Musketeers*. D'Artagnan, Aramis, Athos and Porthos accompany us as we ascend.

We encounter other literary figures as we tour the house. There is Uncas, the Last of the Mohicans, and the Pathfinder, another of Fennimore Cooper's heroes from the pioneering days of US history. Rip van Winkle and Hester Prynne are two more beautifully carved characters that adorn this treasure chest of a riverside dwelling. But, perhaps most spectacular is the frieze in carved oak by Thomas Nicholls which shows eighty-two scenes from some of Shakespeare's plays such as *Othello*, *Macbeth*, *Antony and Cleopatra* and others. Throughout the house other literary and historical characters can be found: Alfred the Great, Robin Hood, Bismarck, the heroines of

No. 2 Temple Place was built by William Waldorf Astor as his family London home. It had every modern convenience – as can be seen by this cherub using his telephone

Arthurian legend such as Elaine, Guinevere and more. The first Viscount Astor was a cultured man and showed his love of learning at 2 Temple Place.

Since the Astors left, the house has had a number of tenants including The Society of Incorporated Accountants and Auditors. In 1983 Richard Hoare of Hoare's Bank set up The Bulldog Trust to generate support for charities and in 1999 the Trust bought 2 Temple Place. In keeping with its history of fine craftsmanship, there now hangs outside a splendid wrought iron sign of a bulldog. So, from the Columbus' caravel, *The Santa Maria*, on the gilded weathervane on the roof that represents American origins, to the very British bulldog on the ground floor exterior, 2 Temple Place is all of a piece, architectural and artistic unity. It's well worth taking a look at this "imposing casket of Portland stone", especially as we don't have to worry about wolves coming down to the river to drink and catch prey. And, a bonus this, The Bulldog Trust, has opened the house, at certain times, to the public. It is to be used for exhibitions that would not normally be at the larger museums or galleries. That's an extra reason for visiting this delightful house.

London's Lobby

Today, Blackheath, the wide and windy 270 acres of upland heath in London's postal district SE3, which is shared by Greenwich and Lewisham, is crossed not only by a busy main road, the A2, but many other minor roads, tracks and paths. Once, the only thoroughfare was Watling Street, the Roman road that went from Dover (Portus Dubris) via Canterbury (Duovernum Canticorum) and Rochester (Dubroviae) to London (Londinium), the capital of the province that lay at the edge of the Empire.

Blackheath has often been called "London's Lobby", the gateway to the capital. The strategically placed high plateau close to the political centre of the country has been the gathering place for many rebellions and celebrations over the centuries. Danish Vikings camped there around 1011-13, during which time they took prisoner and murdered Alphege, Archbishop of Canterbury, who offered himself as ransom for his people. He was battered to death with the bones left over from a meal they had just eaten. Hawksmoor's glorious baroque church in Greenwich is dedicated to the saint.

In the summer of 1381 Wat Tyler assembled the anti-poll tax rebels of Kent on the Heath as part of the Peasants' Revolt before he marched on London and died at the hands of the

Blackheath – Morden College "for poor merchants" founded is 1695

The Ranger's House, Blackheath – seen from Greenwich Park

Mayor, William Walworth, in front of the 14 year-old boy king, Richard II. It was another of the rebel leaders, the vagrant, egalitarian priest, John Ball, who composed the lines:

> When Adam delved and Eve span,
> Who was then the gentleman?

The Revolt failed and he, too, was executed. Taxes are still with us, but thankfully while some of us might lose our heads metaphorically about their oft time iniquity, we don't do so literally.

Another anti-taxation revolt was led by the Irishman, Jack Cade, in 1450 during the reign of Henry VI when 20,000 men gathered at Blackheath before going on to defeat the royal forces at Sevenoaks, and later to occupy London. The rebels dispersed after being promised reforms and pardons. Cade, however, was captured, tortured and killed. So much for the word of our leaders. It was ever thus. Let us move on before I sound too cynical about politicians.

After his famous victory at Agincourt in 1415, when a French army vastly superior in numbers was defeated, mainly by the Welsh archers use of the long bow, Shakespeare's Hal, King Henry V, received a tumultuous welcome by thousands on Blackheath. Though he gained much of France and Catherine of Valois as his wife, he died only seven years later at the early age of 35. His widow, against opposition from Parliament, secretly married Owen Tudor and their grandson, Henry VII, was the first Tudor king of England. So us Taffs are good at other things than just rugby and singing, we can found a glorious dynasty too.

Blackheath Village – the Reminiscence Centre – full of local and living history – well worth a visit

Blackheath also played its part in the marital see-saw of King Henry VIII's life, for it was there that he went to meet his fourth wife, Anne of Cleeves, whose somewhat flattering portrait had been commissioned by Thomas Cronmwell. The King was so disappointed by plain, homely Anne that he uncharitably called her, "My Flanders Mare". Plain or not, Anne was at least one of the Royal ogre's wives to survive. She was divorced with a pension of £3,000 and various properties. Cromwell didn't fare so well – he was executed.

The Stuarts, too, had associations with the Heath. Mary, Queen of Scots' son, James I, brought with him to the English court not only followers but the game of golf and it was on the Heath that it was introduced to England. A

Society of Blackheath Golfers – the Royal Blackheath Golf Club (the oldest golf club in England) was formed in 1608 and the wearing of a red coat while playing on the course became obligatory. Eventually, increasing urbanisation of the area caused the club to amalgamate with Eltham Golf Club in 1923.

When the Stuart line was restored after the regicide government of Oliver Cromwell and the Interregnum (1649-1660), James I's grandson, Charles II, was greeted by a huge welcoming crowd on Blackheath as he made his way to London from exile on the continent. No doubt, they were fed up with the joyless repression of Britain's only experiment so far with a republican government.

The Heath was not a place to cross alone at night, for there were footpads and highwaymen operating. Those felons who were caught often ended up on the gibbet, their bodies swinging in the wind and their flesh pecked away by scavenging birds. Samuel Pepys records in his famous diary such "a filthy sight" as he made his way to Shooters Hill.

It wasn't until towards the end of the eighteenth century that residential development began and there are some fine old houses around the Heath. In the north-west corner, backing onto Greenwich Park, is Ranger's House. This was originally Chesterfield House, the home of Phillip Stanmore, 4th Earl of Chesterfield, author of the famous *Letters to My Son*. He claimed that from his home one could see the noblest views of London. Would that it were so now but they are long gone; the capital has expanded up to and way beyond the grand 1748 house.

In 1815 the house became Ranger's House, the official residence of the Ranger of Greenwich Park. In 1807 the Duchess of Brunswick had moved there to be near her daughter Caroline who, in 1795, had married George III's son, the Prince of Wales. After the birth of their daughter, Princess Charlotte, they separated and Caroline moved to Montague House on the Heath (since demolished) where she lived an infamous private life, which was the subject of *A Delicate Investigation* in 1806 (the delicacy stemmed from the fact it was the Queen's sexual activity that was being investigated). When the Prince of Wales became King George IV in 1820 she was offered £50,000 to renounce her title of Queen and live abroad. She refused and on Coronation Day, July 19th, 1821, she tried to enter Westminster Abbey but was prevented, much to her chagrin and that of a large number of the public who supported her. When she died there were soon riots between the opposing factions of the King and his deceased wife.

Ranger's House is now administered by English Heritage and is home to the Wernher Collection of more than 650 works of art, medieval and renaissance paintings, pottery, jewellery and sculpture, all well worth visiting but I wouldn't have minded meeting Queen Caroline, she sounds like someone who liked a fight, a spirited woman.

Across the Heath, in the south-east corner is The Paragon, designed by Michael Serles and built during 1793-1807. This elegant Georgian crescent of fourteen very large semi-detached houses linked by Tuscan colonnades is a grand architectural statement which pleases the eye: something that can't often be said by some of today's monstrosities.

Next to The Paragon are the beautiful grounds and handsome buildings of Morden College, the foundation of which in 1695 is a tale worth telling. Sir John Morden, a prosperous merchant based in Aleppo, made his fortune in the East. He was a member of both the Turkey Company and the East India Company. Having been successful in his ventures, he decided to return home. He packed all his wealth in three ships and went ahead of them to London. He reached home but his ships did not and Sir John faced penury. However, months later, his ships put safely into port after having been forced off course by a dreadful storm. His fortune was restored. Having a philanthropic nature and no children, he decided to found "a college for poor merchants" who had fallen on hard times. The result was Morden College, designed, it is claimed, by Sir Christopher Wren and with carvings in the chapel attributed to Grinling Gibbons.

Blackheath Village did not really develop until the railway arrived in 1849, when there was rapid development from two cottages and no church or parish to the trendy area it is today. The Heath still plays its part in local life: on weekends football matches are played there, kites are flown, donkeys are ridden alongside Duke Humphrey's Road and, once a year, there is a gathering of thousands, spectators and participants, for the London Marathon which starts there, at the gateway to the capital, "London's Lobby".

Fulham Palace and its Gardens

In his diary entry for October 11th, 1681, John Evelyn the English diarist, courtier and garden designer wrote: "I went to Fulham to visit the Bishop of London: in whose Garden I first saw the 'Sedum arborescens' in flower which was exceedingly beautiful". Evelyn was an expert on trees and his book *Sylva or a Discourse on Trees* was a standard textbook for hundreds of years. His diary (which was discovered in an old clothes basket at his brother's home in 1817) has other references to Fulham, so what is there to excite such interest?

Fulham lies in a loop on the north bank of the River Thames opposite Barnes and Putney. It is in the London Borough of Hammersmith and Fulham which, although one of the smaller metropolitan boroughs at 1,617 hectares, has one of the highest population densities, 157,000 reside there. Because of its closeness to such places as Chelsea and Kensington, it is included in the list of prime London areas and property prices reflect this. The average asking price of all property in the SW6 area was £992,260 at the time of printing.

Fulham has other claims to fame. Do you remember the 1976 film *The Omen* about a boy, Damien, possessed by the Devil? One of the characters, Father Brennan, is impaled by a lightning conductor when it falls from the spire of a church that was struck by lightning. Well, the church was All Saints, Fulham, at the north-west end of Putney Bridge. Danish invaders wintered at Fulham in 879; the Earl of Essex pursued Charles I across a makeshift bridge of boats at Fulham; and during the eighteenth century, the area had a reputation for debauchery, with prostitution and gambling being the main attractions. Some dictionaries define a "Fulham" as loaded dice. Today the main draws are the two Premiership football clubs that lie within the borough, Fulham and Chelsea. Say no more.

Fulham Palace has been called "London's best kept secret" It was the official country residence of the Bishops of London from the eleventh century to 1973 and while the present brick manor house dates from the sixteenth century, there are older parts. At one time, when the Palace stood on the river's edge, before it was embanked, there was a moat surrounding it, which was the longest in England. Signs of Neolithic and Roman settlements have also been found.

It is for its trees that Fulham Palace became famous. At one time, when John Evelyn first visited them, he recorded, sadly, that "the Bishop of London did cutte-down a noble Clowd of trees at Fulham". However, Henry Compton, Bishop in 1675, was banished there for two years in 1686 by King James II for being anti-Catholic and began the planting which was to make the gardens a place to visit if you had arboriculture interests. He introduced the American magnolia, azalea, and red horse chestnut to England. The first coffee tree was grown in his heated "stoves". Some of his introductions can still be found in the gardens, which originally covered more than 30 acres

Fulham Palace, London, official residence of the Bishop of London until 1973

(though sadly only 12 remain now). The most venerable of the trees is The Fulham Palace Holm Oak which, at around 500 years of age, predates the time of Bishop Compton. This example of Quercus ilex is found in a recumbent position in a shady corner of the garden by the boundary wall (Wouldn't you like a lie down after 500 years?). It has been rightly honoured by being classified as one of the Great Trees of London.

When Evelyn visited in 1681 the grounds were obviously remarkable enough to warrant inclusion in his diary. The Bishop exchanged seeds with William Penn in America and became Deputy Superintendent of the Royal Gardens and one of the commissioners for Trade and Plantations. No doubt, such connections enabled him to indulge his sylvan interest that we can still appreciate today.

The Palace and grounds are run by a Trust and a restoration project has renovated the building and the Bishops' Park. The walled garden with its spectacular wisteria, herb knot-garden and vineries are also being restored. Do look for the Bishops'

This is the oldest part of Fulham Palace, the Fizjames Quadrangle.

Tree carved by the environmental sculptor Andrew Frost – various bishops have been carved out of cedar wood and applied to the huge Cedar of Lebanon which is in the North Garden. There you will find Bishop Porteus, a campaigner for the abolition of slavery; Bishop Creighton, an historian of note; Bishop Bonner a catholic who, some claim, tortured Protestant prisoners that he kept in the Palace lock-up; and there is a bench with Bishop Compton having a snooze.

The large area of meadow behind the walled garden is full of wild flowers in spring and there are kinetic sculptures by Peter Logan to add interest throughout the year.

One last interesting piece of information about Fulham Palace is that it is on the Buckingham Palace Ley Line. What, you might ask, is a ley line? It is an alignment of ancient sites that represent linear streams of an unknown energy type that is beneficial to living things. It seems to work for the all the plants in the gardens and our present monarch and her consort are both hale and hearty at their advanced ages. So, scoff on, sceptics.

From Shimla to the South Circular

The top deck of a London bus is a wonderful vantage point from which to see sights of the capital that you might otherwise miss. Coming along the A215, the Norwood Road in Tulse Hill, heading south towards Crystal Palace on the No. 68, my bus got stuck in the usual traffic jam at the junction with the South Circular Road. As we inched along I looked out of the window and saw, in front of a large double-fronted Victorian house, a sign almost hidden by foliage, which said, "South London Botanical Institute Open to the Public".

I determined to visit this newly-found (to me, at least), intriguing edifice and, fortunately, did so on a Thursday which is the only day it is open to the public, from 10 a. m. – 4 p. m. (though appointments to visit on other days can be made by arrangement). What I found was worth the visit as was the story of the man behind it.

Allan Octavian Hume (1829-1912), of Scottish descent, was one of those redoubtable individuals who not only helped build "the Empire on which the sun never set" but, unlike many of those who saw India, his field of action, simply as a means of enriching themselves, he also gave something back, so much so that in 1985, seventy-three years after his death, the Indian Government featured him on a series of postage stamps commemorating the founding of the Indian National Congress, a singular honour indeed, as he appeared beside Gandhi, Nehru, and the other greats in the history of Indian independence.

Hume trained as a doctor and as such went out to India to join the Bengal Civil Service in Calcutta, but he was not the typical sahib. He proved a successful administrator with liberal views, introducing free primary school education in the town under his jurisdiction. He rose and became Director General of Agriculture, but his reformist policies did not go down well with many of his colleagues for although he was "untainted by racism" many of them were not. They saw his attempts at improving the lives of the rural poor as mistaken. He paid for his enlightenment by being demoted. Hume spent 45 years attempting to promote agricultural reform, which he saw as being essential for India's development.

Another of his contributions to Indian culture was as an ornithologist. He became an expert on the subcontinent's bird-life. His extensive and important collection was housed in Rothney Castle, his palatial residence in Shimla. Much of it is now at the Natural History Museum at Tring.

But it is as a founder of the Indian National Congress in 1885, which fought for greater share in government by Indians and eventual independence, that he is best remembered in that country. The INC became one of the two major political parties in India and after 1947 and the end of The Raj, it became the dominant political party.

When Hume returned to England after 45 years, he turned his attention to horticulture and began to study British flora.

The notice on Norwood Rd, Tulse Hill, which attracted my attention.

Such was his enthusiasm that in 1909 he bought a large Victorian house in Tulse Hill which, a year later, opened as the South London Botanical Institute – a sanctuary where both professional and amateur botanists could pursue their interest and exchange information and specimens.

It is a splendid place where anyone with an interest in plants can study in an environment that has changed little from Hume's day. Beside the library with its historic collection of journals and reference guides, there is a herbarium with over a hundred thousand examples of lichens, fungi, algae, and plants from all over Europe and the British Isles. In the garden behind the Institute there are medicinal plants, poisonous ones, and collections of ferns and wild flowers. The pond with its wildlife is a favourite with the school children who visit, but it is not as popular as the insect-eating plants such as the Venus flytrap. It is good to see children take an interest in the natural world, especially when they come from heavily urbanised areas where they have little chance to see flowers and other plants growing in conditions foreign to their own lives.

There is a wide selection of courses held both in the Institute and on field trips. Lectures, workshops, walks and courses are held, with something of interest for everyone. You can go on a "Fungus Foray", join a "Plant Dyeing Workshop", explore a "Summer Tree Course", or take part in "The Big Botanical Draw". All of these inspire a love of plants in young people and help others to maintain their interest.

Allan Octavian Hume has a lot to be thanked for, as has the No. 68 bus, for although it is a long way from Shimla to the South Circular Road, without a traffic hold-up on the latter, I would never have discovered this fascinating place nor the volunteers who maintain it. Thank you.

It's well-worth a visit and drop something in the collection box for it is a charity dependent on membership fees, a generous grant from the City Bridge Trust, and donations from visitors.

Homes R Us

Many of the Roman roads of Londinium are still in use today as modern highways. Ermine Street is now the A10, lying beneath Bishopsgate and leading north to what were once the King's hunting grounds beyond Shoreditch and Hoxton, hence its name at one point, Kingsland Road. For centuries this was countryside: small farms, hamlets, private, and market gardens and nurseries.

These rural surroundings remained until the proximity of the growing City of London made it an attractive place for the rich and powerful to build houses. The clean, fresh air also made it suitable for the continuation of a tradition that started in medieval times – charitable endowments such as schools and almshouses by City Livery companies and their philanthropic members. Sir Robert Geffrye, Lord Mayor of London and Master of one of the Great Twelve Companies – The Ironmongers' Company – left a bequest in 1714 for the construction of almshouses for ironmongers' widows originally, but eventually for 56 pensioners and widows (four to each of the sixteen dwellings).

The two-storey group of cottages forms three sides of a tranquil courtyard. In the centre is a chapel above the entrance to which stands a statue of the benefactor, Sir Robert Geffrye.

A fine avenue of lime trees makes this oasis all the more welcoming. Although the area was heavily bombed during the Second World War, the museum escaped major damage. However, the iron railings and gate along the road were taken for the war effort, and were only replaced in 1973 by the then Greater London Council.

Before the First World War, the Ironmongers' Company sold the elegant and simple Grade 1 listed building to the London Council and from 1919-1914 it was converted into a museum. The first floors were removed, as were the stairs and many party-walls and a sequence of small galleries was created. Whereas the area had once been famous for horticulture, as it became more populous and built-up, it became the furniture-making centre of the capital. It was therefore decided to illustrate the history of the industry by turning the almshouses into a museum of domestic interiors from 1600 to the twentieth century. You can see fully-furnished rooms from Elizabethan times to the 1950's, from the heavily-panelled Jacobean to the light and airy modern. As we progress from one room to the next, we move from candlelight to paraffin lamps, gaslight and electricity, and as domestic comfort increased, from log-fires to central heating. To the delight of many visitors, they can recognise in the later rooms not only their parents family homes but often that of their grandparents. The Geffrye must be the only British museum that charts the history of middle-class domestic interiors, for we do not find there the houses of the very poor or the very rich.

But it is not only the inside rooms that attract us for, as a complement to them, period garden rooms have also been

The Geffryes Museum, Shoreditch (left) – above the main entrance is this statue (right) of the founder, Sir Robert Geffryes, Lord Mayor of London and Master of the Ironmongers' Company

created behind the museum, based on research into the constantly changing nature of gardens. They start with a Knot Garden, a favourite of the 1550's, with its interlocking pattern based on a panel of a cupboard in the Elizabethan Room. Such gardens were meant to be seen from above, from inside the house, where their intricacy would have been appreciated.

The garden "rooms" continue through Elizabethan, Jacobean, Georgian, Victorian and Edwardian. The herbaceous borders of the latter and the profusion of old-fashioned flowers found in cottage gardens remain popular today.

The award-winning Herb Garden, made from scratch on a derelict site next to the museum, is an aromatic heaven for all visitors whether human, animal or insect. In such an urban area it is a happy reminder of the time Shoreditch was "a green and pleasant land" and Hoxton a famous centre of horticulture.

In the 12 formally laid out beds there are nearly 200 herbs, many of which have been in use since medieval times and some of which, such as fennel, were brought here by the Roman Legions. There are culinary herbs, tarragon and lovage, for example; medicinal herbs such as comfrey, feverfew, and the different mints which aid digestion; household herbs such as mugwort which deters moths; and cosmetic herbs such as cowslip which, it was once thought, if mixed with white wine and used as a wash, would get rid of wrinkles. Many dyes were once produced from plants such as woad and madder, and these too have their place. In the bed for salad herbs we find familiar ingredients such as chicory, as well as the less-widely used marshmallow and hops. There's a special bed for bee plants with golden rod, nettle, and many others, for without these industrious visitors all our gardens would be much worse off.

South-facing and sheltered by brick walls, two of which date from the eighteenth century, the micro-climate of the Herb Garden ensures a wind-free environment for plants and animals. No wonder that in 1992 the garden won the London Spade Award for excellence in the development and use of open spaces in London.

Plans are afoot to further develop the museum into one which shows The History of the Home, a major change which would make it a centre for learning and discovery, not just about the physical nature of the home but also those intangibles, the ideas and values which go into the fabric of a family home. The Heritage Lottery Fund has already given a starter grant and it is hoped to get more from various sources. It would be fitting if all could be up-and-running by 2014, for it was in 1714 that the almshouses were built and 1914 that the museum was opened. Two reasons for celebrating.

Next time you're heading up the A10, stop for a while and do yourself a favour, visit the Geffrye Museum.

Snail Mail and Rowland Hill

We've come a long way since messages were sent in a cleft stick carried by a runner. In these days of email, Skype and other means of electronic communication, it is easy to forget how revolutionary "snail mail" was and the debt we owe to Sir Rowland Hill (1795-1879), the originator of penny postage.

The history of the post is chequered. Henry VIII had a Master of Posts who maintained a regular service but only on the main roads from London. Innkeepers provided horses and passed the mail to the next post along the way. Originally, there was no postal service for the public, only the King's letters and Foreign Posts but in 1653 the first public post was established. There was no local delivery, post had to be picked up from a central point, and the system was slow. Mail coaches started in 1784, revolutionizing delivery, but they declined with the arrival of the railway.

Hill was born in 1795 in Kidderminster, Worcestershire, where his father ran a private and, for the times, radical school which had no corporal punishment, developed scientific and artistic enquiry and was run to a great extent by the pupils themselves. Hill became a teacher there, carrying on his father's novel approach to education and, eventually, becoming a publisher of cheap, good-quality educational books

Rowland Hill (1795-1879), the originator of the penny postage – suitably flanked by post boxes. This bronze statue by Edward Onslow Ford now stands outside the General Post Office in King Edward Street in the City of London but it was originally erected outside the Royal Exchange and unveiled by Edward, Prince of Wales on June 7th, 1882. It was moved to its current location in 1923.

His interests were varied, including Robert Owen's socialistic schemes and the colonization of Southern Australia but it was the Government's commission to consider postal reform that really fired him. The biggest drawback of the existing system was that it was the addressee who had to pay for the delivery and many couldn't or wouldn't pay. In 1837 Hill published a pamphlet entitled *Post Office Reform and its Importance and Practicability*, which gained him notice and huge public support.

His idea was "a cheap and standard charge, prepaid and carried on a bit of paper large enough to bear a stamp and covered at the back with a glutinous wash". Simplicity itself. No wonder it was popular with many for at one time it could cost a workman almost half a day's wages to send a letter. Even so, there were those in authority who opposed his scheme because they feared a drop in revenue. Nevertheless, in 1840 a uniform Penny Post was introduced.

The scheme was a great success. The number of letters sent rose from 72,000 in 1840 to 208,000 in 1842. Doubting Thomases were silenced, especially when they saw the revenue increase dramatically. Delivery times improved also: a letter which in 1830 took 6 months to reach India, took only 40 days in 1850. Domestic postal delivery also sped up and instead of taking weeks to reach a distant part of Great Britain, it would often take only days. Within a few decades the idea of the Penny Post had spread around the world. Hill would have been astonished to learn that at one time, when sending letters, packets and parcels was at its height, the Post Office railway moved 50,000 bags of mail beneath the streets of London.

In 1846 Hill became Secretary to the Post Office and made further innovations. He reformed the Money Order Office and the Packet Service. However, in 1864 he had to retire because of ill-health but even then his sense of public duty did not cease for, in 1867, he published a report recommending nationalisation of the railways, a brave suggestion in those days when such measures were anathema to many politicians, some of whom had a vested interest in maintaining the status quo.

When Sir Rowland Hill died in 1867, he was so popular that a memorial appeal for funds for a commemorative statue raised over £16,000, a huge sum, much more than was needed. When the statue was finally paid for, the residue was spent on the welfare of postal workers, on benefits for the sick and out of work. The bronze statue by the young artist Edward Onslow Ford was finally unveiled by H. R. H. The Prince of Wales on June 7th, 1882, in front of the Royal Exchange in the heart of the City of London, a place that benefited greatly by his postal reforms. It moved to its present position outside the General Post Office in 1923.

In the summer, not long after Prince Edward's unveiling of the statue in its original position, children were seen sticking stamps on it, an affectionate tribute to the man who inaugurated the Penny Post.

Crocodiles, Pelicans and a Boozy Elephant

When standing on the Blue Bridge that crosses the Lake in St. James's Park and looking either west towards Buckingham Palace or at the splendid view east over Horse Guards Parade and the towers and pinnacles of Whitehall and beyond, towards the London Eye on the South Bank, it is difficult to imagine this place as a disease-infested swamp, which it once was, with St. James's Hospice for Leper Women at its northern edge, whose saint gave his name to the area. Low-lying, it was subject to frequent flooding by the Thames and Tyburn Brook. Today, it is the oldest of London's eight Royal parks and its attractive 58 acres make it one of the most popular with Londoners and tourists alike.

It was Henry VIII who began to change this desolate area. He bought it off Eton College, drained much of it and established it for deer coursing and duck shooting. The leper hospice was demolished and the palace we now see there, St. James's, at which Court ambassadors are accredited, was built in what has become the familiar red-brick Tudor style we see at Hampton Court and, closer, the gate house to Lambeth Palace. The monarchs had yet to move across the park for the palace they now inhabit, Buckingham Palace, had not been built.

A pelican in St. James' Park

The Royal association was continued by Elizabeth I who was also fond of the chase and carried on her father's pastime, frequently hunting and holding tournaments as well as other entertainments in what had once been a swamp. The first Stuart monarch, James I, improved the water supply and established a menagerie in the park: there were exotic creatures such as crocodiles and an elephant that was given a gallon of wine each day. Goodness knows what state the poor beast was in when in "must". Dangerous, I should think, for there was no other elephant on which to exhaust its lust.

James was also fond of birds and established an aviary in what is now Birdcage Walk, down which until 1828 only the Royal family and the Hereditary Grand Falconer could drive their carriages. Gone are the cassowaries and parakeets, replaced by graceful eighteenth century houses and the Wellington Barracks. Friendly soldiers have long been associated with both St. James's Park and Green Park.

James's second son, King Charles I, did little to the park and I'm sure paid it scant attention as he walked through to his execution outside the Banqueting Hall in Whitehall on January 30th, 1649, a cold winter's day.

With the end of the regicide government of the Interregnum in 1660, the fortunes of the Park picked up. Charles II, having spent much of his youth in Paris returned from the French capital with grand ideas, no doubt inspired by Versailles and the court of the Sun King. He had the park completely redesigned with a long formal body of water where the swamp once was, in which the Merry Monarch would swim in summer and skate on when it froze in winter.

He, too, was fond of birds and the Russian Ambassador gave him some pelicans to adorn the new lake in the gardens designed by the French landscape artist, André Mollet. The Royal bird collection also boasted a crane with a wooden leg. Charles even made one of his French favourites, the poet Saint-Evremond, the Governor of Duck Island. It is not known if the poet realised that his territory was the small island in the middle of the lake in St. James's Park. The Doge of Venice gave Charles two gondolas for his new canal and gondoliers to go with them. Unfortunately, the King neglected to pay them so they returned soon after to the Adriatic republic from whence they came.

Charles brought with him from his continental exile a game, a kind of cross between croquet and bowls, called Pele-Mele from which the land on the north side of the park derived the name Pall Mall.

He opened the park to the public and it became a fashionable place to take the air and be seen. Charles, himself, would stroll there with Nell Gwynn, one of his many mistresses. The popular monarch was not the only one to use the Park for his amorous pastimes and eventually it became known as a haunt for whores and duellists and a place where all kinds of depravity took place. John Wilmot, the libertine Earl of Rochester, wrote in his *A Ramble in St. James's Park:*

> "When I, who still take care to see
> Drunkenness relieved by lechery,
> Went out into St. James's Park
> to cool my head and fire my heart…"

And these are some of the milder lines from that poem.

The Park as we see it today is mainly the work of George IV's favourite architect, John Nash, who, among other changes, made the body of water more like a natural lake by joining Duck Island to the mainland. He also built on it the incongruous-looking Swiss cottage for the Keeper of the Royal Birds, which later became the headquarters of the Ornithological Society of London. It now houses the London Historic Parks and Gardens Trust.

For over two hundred years cows were pastured in the Park, near Whitehall, and the successive old ladies who acted as milkmaids made a nice living from selling milk straight from the udder. When, at the beginning of the Twentieth Century it was proposed that they be got rid of, there was much public outcry. Even the King, Edward VII, spoke up in the milkmaids' favour, claiming that he himself as a child had enjoyed milk from their cows but eventually, in 1905, officialdom won its way and the few remaining cows were banished, the milkmaids pensioned off and Admiralty Arch built where Londoners and tourists had once enjoyed a simple pleasure. It seems a shame that small attractions like that should be got rid of, in what is, after all, London's oldest and prettiest Royal Park.

A Passion for Collecting

I wouldn't mind betting that if a vote was taken as to which was the best-loved and most popular of London's museums, the Horniman Museum would come out near the top. The British Museum is grand; those in "Albertopolis" have their dinosaurs and earthquake machines; and the Imperial War Museum can be too poignant but there, on top of Forest Hill in London SE23, is the one that is most full of life and children.

The Horniman began a few miles away, in Croydon, where John Horniman, tea merchant, had his home at Coombe Cliff, a large Victorian house with extensive grounds. He came from a Quaker family, wore traditional Quaker garb and rode his horse to work. It seems that he was the first to sell tea in packets, thus establishing the popularity of his product and making his fortune.

John Horniman had a passion for collecting and would bring back exotic artefacts from his travels to tea plantations around the world. He passed the collecting bug on to his son, Frederick, who filled his home on the crest of Forest Hill with his finds to such an extent that his poor wife gave him the choice of "Walrus or me". He solved this unenviable conundrum by building a new house and, in a spirit of philanthropy and education for all, opened his old home to the public three

The Horniman Museum in Forest Hill

times a week as a free museum. Although somewhat distant from the city, over eighty thousand people came to see the gift the MP and tea merchant had made to the Victorian public.

So popular did the museum become that Horniman employed the Arts and Crafts architect C. Harrison Townsend (who also designed the Bishopsgate Institute and the Whitechapel Gallery) to design a purpose-built museum. Standing in such a prominent position amid sixteen acres of beautifully kept gardens which have recently been remodelled, the distinctive stone and red-brick building was the result, with its abundance of relief ornament and the large, colourful mosaic on the main facade by Robert Anning Bell, a member of the Artworkers' Guild, which is an allegory on the course of human life. Over 100,000 pieces of terrazzo went into its making, all applied by young women who had the delicate touch that Bell insisted upon. The Horniman has been called "the only pure art nouveau building in London". It is testament to the success of the museum that in 2001 an extension very much in the style of the original was added, to join the splendid Victorian conservatory from Coombe Cliff, which had been dismantled and re-erected nearby almost as homage to the begetter of the original collection.

Not only did John Horniman inherit his father's collecting mania but also a touch of his streak of eccentricity, for John would eat rice pudding at least once a day every day, no matter where in the country he was. Even as a Devon MP he had his puddings with him on his journey around his constituency.

This excellent small museum has an extensive natural history section that gives a comprehensive account of the living world, including evolutionary development, a subject that was a source of much controversy in Victorian times. The birds and animals, especially the gigantic walrus, are favourites with visitors, particularly the children. Often there are school groups sketching or doing projects there. The thriving education department has links with many schools and colleges and it encourages visits. Artists-in-residence have produced vibrant work with pupils, including dry work inspired by the delicate sand painting made by the Navajo Indians of Arizona, which shows their interpretation of the world.

The aquarium, too, is popular and innovative, illustrating not only marine life but the threat of pollution to the aquatic environment. Looking after our world receives much attention and can be seen in the rich ethnographic collection, which is

The conservatory of the Horniman Museum. It originally stood at Horniman House but was transferred here. It was used for concerts, displays etc.

consulted by researchers and is a source of artistic inspiration to visitors. As is another department, the collection of musical instruments from many ages and countries. This is of world renown, consulted by researchers from all over the globe.

One of the most popular exhibitions of recent years was the "African Worlds" exhibition, which "offered glimpses of Africa seen through the eyes of artists, divines, anthropologists, drummers, elders and exiles." The guiding principal behind the exhibition was that there is not one Africa but many where, over thousands of years, civilizations have flourished: think of Kemet (Ancient Egypt), Axum (Ethiopia), Benin and Zimbabwe. All this was brought to life by audio-visual displays. In our multicultural society today it is worth remembering that other such cultures have contributed to ours.

The journey to Forest Hill is well worth making, especially if you take the kids. And don't forget the farm in the grounds and the lovingly kept gardens where you can have a picnic as you enjoy the spectacular view of London.

Drunk for a Penny, Dead Drunk for Two Pence

"In the Fields? What fields?" the puzzled visitor might ask as he looks around him at the maze of streets and alleyways that lie in the shadow of Centre Point at this busy crossroad in London WC2. Then he might turn and look at the noticeboard that stands in front of the Palladian style church that Henry Flitcroft built between 1730 and 1734 and observe, in gold lettering on a red background, that the first church on the site was built in 1101 by Queen Matilda, wife of King Henry I. "Ah, that's why it's called St. Giles-in-the- Fields. No doubt in those days there were fields." And he's right, because before many outlying villages were swallowed up in the maw of the metropolis, the scene would have been more bucolic than urban. There are other examples where the names give us clues of a rural past: think of St. Martin-in-the Fields, Moorfields and Smithfield.

The Parish of St. Giles-in-the-Fields is roughly a triangle formed by three main highways: New Oxford Street, Shaftesbury Avenue, and Charing Cross Road. It was originally a small village outside London, ideally situated for the leper hospital and the attached chapel, established by good Queen Matilda in 1101 and dedicated to St. Giles, patron saint of lepers and

The Resurrection Gate (left) at which prisoners heading for Tyburn were given "St. Giles Cup" - a jug of ale to help them on their way to the gallows. Henry Flitcroft's St. Giles-in-the-fields (right), completed in 1734 - seen from Phoenix Gardens.

cripples (there's also St. Giles Cripplegate in the Barbican in the Square Mile of the City which bears this out). The lazaretto remained as such until the fifteenth century when it opened its doors to those who were just infirm or poor.

The church is one of the most handsome Georgian churches in London, and has much of interest for the visitor. It includes the pulpit from West Street Chapel where John and Charles Wesley preached and memorials to the poet Andrew Marvell who was also assistant to Milton and George Chapman (the translator of classical poems whose *Homer* inspired Keats to write of "travelling in realms of gold" and "standing silent upon a peak in Darien"). It has seen much suffering since beginning as a refuge for lepers.

The Great Plague of 1665 started in the parish and, it is claimed, one hundred thousand perished in that unusually hot summer. Prisoners heading from Newgate Jail in the City to Tyburn Tree, the gallows, at the junction of what is now Bayswater Road and Edgware Road, had to pass nearby and at the Resurrection Gate of the church where they were given "St. Giles' cup", a jug of ale to help them on their way to their pitiful end, a tradition that continued for some time.

Perhaps the most famous person to end up on the nearby gallows was Sir John Oldcastle, a leader of the Lollards (early precursors of Protestantism who wanted reforms in the Catholic Church). He served under King Henry IV and was an intimate friend of his son, the Prince of Wales, who later became King Henry V. Sounds familiar? It should. Shakespeare used him as a model for the larger than life figure of Falstaff in *King Henry IV, Parts One and Two*, *The Merry Wives of Windsor*, and he's mentioned in *Henry V*. When Oldcastle was hanged and his scaffold was set alight in 1417, it is claimed that he cursed the king and his descendants. He also laid a blight on the surrounding area, which many say accounts for the decline of the parish in the years to come.

Such was its decline that St. Giles' Rookery, as it became called, was one of the worst slums in the capital. The population of the parish grew to more than 30,000 by 1831. Prostitution and thievery were rife and the place became a breeding ground for squalor and crime. Henry Fielding, the eighteenth century author of *Tom Jones*, was also a barrister and in his *Enquiry in to the Causes of the Late Increase of Robbers* blamed much of it on –"the destruction of all morality, decency and modesty" where there was eternal "swearing whoredom and drunkenness". Even his small force of "thief-takers" was afraid of entering the area. Walter Thornbury in his *Haunted London* (1865) claimed to have seen a public house that bore the sign "Here you may get drunk for a penny, dead drunk for twopence and straw for nothing".

The main means of getting drunk was gin, which was cheaper than ale and imported liberally from Holland following the accession of William of Orange to the English throne in 1689 Perhaps one of the best known of William Hogarth's engravings is *Gin Lane*, set in St. Giles Rookery, where a gin-sodden mother is so drunk she lets her baby fall to its death amid a scene of squalor and debauchery. It was claimed that one house in four was a gin shop where vagrants and the poor could buy oblivion. But the poverty, misery and ruin continued. The Gin Act of 1736 attempted to put an end to all this, but the mob would not accept it and it was not until many of the gin-shops were suppressed by The Sale of Spirits Act in 1751 that the craze for the drink began to wane.

Thankfully, those days of 18th and 19th century drunkenness and depravity have passed. Since the 1950s the area has changed greatly. The population has diminished and there has been clearance of buildings and erection of new ones such as Centre Point and Central St. Giles. However, the area is still worth a visit, not simply for the beautiful church and its historic memorials but also for the Phoenix Gardens nearby where you can sit in quietness amid the city's busyness and spare a thought for those poor folk who lived their short, meagre lives there in days gone by.